The Country and People of Siam

Karl Döhring

The Country and People of Siam

Karl Döhring

Translated

by

Walter E. J. Tips

With a Foreword by
Krisana Daroonthanom

White Lotus Press

This book was originally dedicated to
Herrn Eduard Cuypers

© 1999 by Walter E. J. Tips. All rights reserved.

Originally published as *Siam. Band 1: Land und Volk*, 1923, Folkwang Verlag G.M.B.H., Darmstadt.

White Lotus Co. Ltd.
G.P.O. Box 1141
Bangkok 10501
Thailand

Telephone: (662) 332-4915 and (662) 741-6288-9
Fax: (662) 741-6607 and (662) 741-6287
E-mail: ande@loxinfo.co.th
Website: http://thailine.com/lotus

Printed in Thailand

ISBN 974-8434-87-7 pbk White Lotus Co. Ltd., Bangkok

Front cover: High-ranking Siamese in theater dress, leading role
Back cover: An oxen carriage, North Siam

Contents

Foreword to the 1999 Edition

The idea of reprinting the original edition of *Siam, Land und Volk* by Karl Döhring, a book of singular interest, deserves warm and full support. The book is an extensive source on of information on Siam (Thailand as of 1939) and the Siamese people around 1900. Foreigners as well as Thais will not only understand Döhring's work but also, and especially, come to an appreciation of the art and culture of old Siam.

The author, an eminent expert on these topics, permits a keen understanding of the life of the Siamese people: their religion, ceremonies, festivities, music, and theatre. The particular circumstances, the way of life, the manners and customs of the Siamese are presented without prejudice, with clear judgement and penetration, and are described in an intuitive, lively, and slightly humorous way. Together with impressive contemporary photographs and remarks, that latter given in an intellectual, mostly impartial but vivid fashion, Döhring introduces the reader from the viewpoint of his wide and scientific horizon to the fascinating world of old Siam, the fabulous kingdom once called the "Country of the White Elephant."

Karl Siegfried Döhring was born on 14 August 1879 in Cologne, the oldest son of the clergyman Carl August Döhring and his wife, *née* Müller-Arns. He was highly inquisitive about a wide number of topics. In 1899, he began studying building at the Royal Technical University in Berlin-Charlottenburg, completing his studies in 1905 with a diploma in architecture. In 1911, he passed the examination for the doctor's degree in architecture at the Royal Technical University of Saxony in Dresden, "with distinction." In 1914, he obtained the doctor of philosophy degree "magna cum laude" in archaeology and the history of art at the Royal University of Bavaria in Erlangen, and, finally, in 1916, he received the doctor's degree in law from the Royal University of Greifswald.

Döhring was fascinated by the abundance of building forms in Farther India. After studies at the University of Berlin, he applied for a post with the Royal Siamese Civil Services in Thailand and in 1906 was appointed Assistant Engineer of the Royal Siamese Railway Department. Promoted Section Engineer in 1907, he planned and supervised the erection of a number of buildings, mostly for the State Railways. More plans for buildings were prepared and completed by Döhring, but presumably only a few were carried out.

In 1909, Döhring was appointed Superintending Architect and Engineer to the Ministry of the Interior and was placed in charge of the Building Section. Immediately after his appointment he was became responsible for two important projects: the town building plan of the residence of the Crown Prince in Phraprathom, and the new royal residence in Petchaburi. His position permitted contacts with his royal employers as well as personal connections with the royal family. In 1909, Prince Dilok Nabarath entrusted the German architect with the erection of his new palace. In September of that year, King Chulalongkorn commissioned Döhring with construction of the palace in Petchaburi and appointed him his First Architect. In 1911, Prince Damrong asked him to build his new palace and Prince Nakhonsavan commissioned a residence for his mother.

In October 1913, Döhring travelled to Germany because of ill health and was never able to return to Siam. While no longer in the Siamese Civil Service, he was nonetheless held in great favor by the King and Princes of Siam. When planning an expedition to northern Siam in 1919, and another in 1929 to the countries of Indian culture, his projects received support, with special invitation and authorization from the Princes Damrong, Mahidol, and Rangsit. King Vajiravudh was an enthusiastic supporter of Döhring's book *Art and Art Industry in Siam*.

After his definitive return to Germany, Döhring abandoned architecture. Between 1912 and 1925 he published four important scientific works and numerous articles on Siamese buildings, art, and culture, and a volume on Indian art. During this period he worked as a freelance designer for industrial production: carpets, tapestry, bronze figures, textiles, and porcelain. In 1919, Döhring, at the zenith of his scientific career, received the title professor. His scientific work received widespread acknowledgement, and he was honored as one of the leading experts on Buddhist architecture. This may have been the turning-point in his professional evolution. His persevering efforts of ten years' duration to realize an expedition to Southeast Asia demonstrate his determination to begin a new career as an art historian and archaeologist. On 1 June 1941, Döhring died in Darmstadt after an operation.

Karl Döhring was a very versatile, productive, and wholly fascinating individual. He was not only a talented architect but an archaeologist and an accomplished art historian. Whatever he turned his hand to, he accomplished with distinction because he devoted his best efforts to his endeavors. The construction of four palaces in Thailand–the palaces for Princes Dilok and Damrong, the residence for the mother of Prince Nakhonsavan (Tamnak Somdej), and the royal palace in Petchaburi (Phra Ram Ratchanivet)–bear witness to his outstanding achievements. With them he proved his eminence as an architect. His most important books in archaeology and art history, *Buddhistische Tempelanlagen in Siam* (1920) and *Art and Art Industry in Siam* (1921) are very well known in Europe and are among the classics on the history of art and architecture in Siam. Professional colleagues, not only in Germany, but in England and France, still quote these books today. Döhring's achievements as an architect are, on the other hand, almost unknown in Europe, but nearly sixty years after his death he remains one of the authorities on Buddhist architecture in Siam.

Dr. Krisana Daroonthanom[1]
Berlin, December 1998

---

[1] Publisher's note. Dr. Krisana Daroonthanom graduated with a Ph.D. on Döhring's work: *Das Architektonische Werk des deutschen Architekten Karl Döhring*, 1998, Universität Osnabrück.

Preface

I spent my most beautiful years in Siam. The old traditions, the inward-looking high culture and the special art, of which the purity of style, the inimitable gracefulness and beauty in design are admirable, became the deepest experience for me. People live simple and naturally there, in an unspoiled carefree life, dedicated to Buddhist religion, and without being embittered by the hard aspects of the struggle for life.

In these three volumes I have attempted to depict the unique character of Siam, without taking into account the latest stage of development of the country which is marked by a similarity to European conditions.

For loaning illustrations I am especially grateful to the Management of the Museums for Ethnography of Berlin, München and Leipzig, as well as to Postmaster Th. Collmann, Consul Karl Zobel, Dr. J. Petri, Dipl.-Ing. Ernst Dorow and Mr. Alfred Schön.

Prof. Dr. Karl Siegfried Döhring
Nürnberg, 5 April 1923

The Country

The old Siamese national coat of arms under King Chulalongkorn[1] showed three fields: a three-headed white elephant on a red background in the top middle part meant Lower Siam, which is inhabited by the Siamese in the strict sense; a white elephant on a yellow field at the bottom left signifies Upper Siam or the Lao States and a Malay *kris* on the lower right points to the Malay Peninsula. The present Kingdom of Siam is not only politically but also geographically subdivided in these three main parts. It lies between the 6th and the 20th degree northern latitude and the 97th and 106th degree eastern longitude. The longest distance from North to South is about 1,640 kilometers, from East to West about 770 kilometers. Siam is about as large as Germany before the War. In the North it is bordered by French Laos and Burma, in the West by Burma and the Gulf of Bengal—part of the Indian Ocean—and in the South from the Malay Federation of States which is under English sovereignty. The Gulf of Siam waters the East Coast of the Malay Peninsula and the South Coast of Siam. In the East the French Indochinese colonies constitute the border, first Cambodia in the South and then French Laos. The Chinese province of Yunnan is separated from Siam by a narrow strip of Burma and French Laos. In this way Siam is squeezed in between English and French colonial possessions.

The three above named parts also constitute three climatically very different areas. In Siam they do not have four different seasons like at home, but three so-called monsoon seasons: the rainy season (*wasanta radu*) from the end of May until October, the cold period (*hemanata radu*) from November until February, and the hot season (*khimhanta radu*) von the middle of February until the end of May. All over Siam the change of seasons is brought about by the monsoon wind. At the end of April the South-South-West monsoon starts. It blows over the seas lying in the South, saturates itself with humidity and thus brings abundant rains to Upper and Lower Siam, as well as to the western side of the Malay Peninsula. In June, July, August and September it rains regularly almost every day for a few hours, while otherwise sunny weather prevails. The rainy season here is not unpleasant as it is in the other tropical areas. In October it rains sparingly. At the beginning of November the South-South-West monsoon and with it the rains stop completely. The wind turns and the North-North-East monsoon starts, which comes from the vast land areas of the Asiatic continent bringing dryness and cold with it. The temperature lowers gradually and at the end of December it reaches its lowest point. During my stay in Bangkok 16 degrees Celsius just before sunrise was the lowest temperature that I observed. From the first half of February it begins to become warmer, the monsoon stops and at the end of April the heat reaches its highest point, about 40-42 degrees Celsius during the hottest part of the days in the afternoon between 1 and 2 p.m. Conversely, on the East Coast of the

Malay Peninsula it rains most in November, December and January, thus during the time of the North-North-East monsoon. The hot period is most unhealthy and causes dangerous tropical diseases such as cholera, dysentery, etc. The beginning of the South-South-West monsoon with its comforting rain is experienced as a great blessing.

The Menam plain is crisscrossed by many canals that are fed more or less by the fresh water of the rivers, especially the Menam. At the end of August the Menam and the other rivers begin to flow over their banks and flood the whole plain. From this is excepted only a strip of some 50 to 60 kilometers on the southern coast, on the northern edge of which lies Bangkok. The flood reaches its greatest height of about 1.5 to 2 meters on average at the beginning of the second half of November. From then onwards the water gradually lowers again. During the inundation the floodwaters are completely opaque and of a yellowish-dark loam color. Only seldom do the floods become so dangerous that the whole harvest is flooded and destroyed. Their height is dependent on the rains. In the Menam plain and in Upper Siam it is on average 120-150 centimeters, while in the southern provinces in the vicinity of Chantabun it reaches a maximum of 250 centimeters. Besides the Menam there are several other rivers, for example the Tachin and the Meklong. The great Mekong constitutes the border between French Laos and Siam. On the peninsula the Petchaburi river is the greatest. Several small rivers flow into the Gulf of Siam.

Due to slowing of the river's flow because of mixing with seawater and additional bonding of salt with mud, the mud sinks at a distance of a few sea miles from the mouth of the Menam. A bar in the river is very bothersome for navigation; during flood tide the water is only five meters deep.

When the rivers carry only small amounts of water during the hot season the brackish water enters from the sea into the canals and makes them unhealthy. During the rainy season the Siamese collect the rainwater in great barrels and all kinds of vessels in order to use it as drinking water during the half-year without rains. If these supplies are finished before the time, then people have to drink the bad water of the brackish canals.[2]

In Upper Siam, which consists mainly of the mountainous areas of the Lao States, the climate is quite mild but shows greater differences in temperature between the hot and cold seasons.

Lower Siam has a maritime climate. The heat of the tropics is softened by the vicinity of the sea so that the average temperature in Bangkok is about 28 degrees Celsius during the rainy season, 30-32 degrees Celsius during the hot period and about 24 degrees Celsius during the cold season.

The northern part of the Malay Peninsula has nearly the same climate as Lower Siam, the southern part on the contrary has the truly tropical climate of the equator countries.

The heat of the Siamese climate is, for the European, very well supportable and very much softened by the monsoon wind, which blows almost all year round. This is helped by wearing lighter dress in the tropics and the fact that after a short stay in the tropics the blood of the European becomes thinner. The Siamese have by nature a thinner blood. The temperature differences between day and night are also smaller than at our latitudes. During the rainy season the temperature is 28 degrees in the morning, rises by noon to 30-32 degrees, lowers in the evening again to 28 degrees and reaches at night a lowest point of 24 degrees Celsius. The climate is very congenial and very salutary especially for people with lung problems.

The mountains of Indochina, which run mostly in a North-South direction and are interrupted by fertile valleys, are more or less spurs of the Himalayas. They fall into two great groups: the western ones first constitute the border between Siam and Burma and then run farther on to the southern Peninsula up to the extreme endpoint in Singapore, while the eastern mountain chain separates the Menam from the Mekong valley. The Menam valley is enclosed between these two great mountain ranges. In terms of fertility it can be compared with Egypt's Nile valley. Every year the Menam inundates the whole of Lower Siam, fertilizes the land with its fertile mud and makes it into one of the richest areas in the world for agriculture. The Menam plain is very flat and rises only a little above sea level. It consists entirely of alluvial soil—loam mixed with some sand—deposited by the river. In deeper layers one still finds the old seabed of mussel lime, sea mussels and sea sand.

The western mountain range which comes out of Yunnan is called the Siamese, the eastern one the Cambodian. In the North of the kingdom several smaller mountain chains split off from the latter and cross through the Lao States. The Siamese mountains are noticeably lower than the Himalayas. The highest peak in the North of the country is Doi Intanon, about 2,500 meters above sea level.

The vast plains of the river valleys are covered with rice fields and horticultural crops while the mountains are covered with forests. In the Lao countries and in the northern provinces as well as on the Korat mountains and some parts of the Malay Peninsula one still finds inaccessible virgin forests which formerly covered the whole country. However, the Siamese have cut down or burned these lusciously growing forests with the continuing development of agriculture in order to gain land for fields. In North Siam one also finds many teak and Sappan[3] forests.

The plains are intersected by many canals, which in southern Siam take the place of overland roads. They not only serve traffic but also, above all, the irrigation of the land. Rice is the main crop of Siam and requires a marshy soil. The best varieties only grow well on flooded fields.

On the edges of the canals, especially near the coast, luscious tropical vegetation reigns. The overhanging bamboo clumps and the numerous high-rising palms with the characteristic line of their silhouettes offer in general beautiful landscape scenes which are enlivened by single houses which spring out from the green of the vegetation of the banks.

Bangkok, the capital of the country, which has not even 900,000 inhabitants today, including all the suburbs, formerly had almost no streets but only canals and therefore people called it the Venice of the East. The southern Siamese are all good oarsmen and very accustomed to the water.

In South Siam, until the construction of the railway line, the traffic was done by boats and merchant ships. The calm current of the Menam and its tributaries is often interrupted by rapids though one can cross over with local boats and ships. In the North, land-traffic is done by ox carts.

The prerequisites for agriculture in Siam are extremely favorable. The great majority of the Siamese are farming people and feed themselves mostly from rice farming. The wealth of the country is growing steadily because by a good harvest a great deal of it can be used for export. Since the people are not very demanding in their needs, exports are higher than imports and wealth grows from year to year during normal times.

Waterways

Because the Siamese are almost exclusively rice farmers and the best rice varieties only grow in marshy river valleys, the majority of the people are concentrated along the waterways. The mountains are all forested and almost uninhabited. Human settlements are not found there; also it is very unhealthy in Siam to live on mountains because of fierce endemic fevers. The houses of the Siamese are pile-dwellings made of wood or bamboo, if possible built on canals so that they partly stand in the water into which they have a direct staircase. Only in the most recent times they have begun with the construction of roads but nevertheless there are no land roads that connect the different greater towns with each other in South Siam. Since the main traffic takes place on the water, the number of boats is extremely high. In Bangkok alone about 600,000 are counted. Every Siamese owns his own boat and the traffic on the canals of Bangkok is very busy. The skill and calm with which the Siamese move ahead even in the greatest throng without hitting each other is admirable. Bastian (*Reisen in Siam*, page 62) already wrote about this: "As much as it is possible things are done on a ship and therefore half of the population of the city always throngs on the Menam or on the branch-canals." On the canals of Bangkok one sees the postman bring their letters by boat; also the monks in their yellow dress let themselves be rowed in boats by their pupils for the collection of alms in the morning. Very lively is the boat traffic in the market areas of the city. On both sides of the river there is a double row of floating houses moored along the banks. Most of these boathouses are sheltering shops. Such boat streets are found in almost all towns. The Siamese love the water very much and one can watch the population bathing on the river banks and on canals almost the whole day. They are very keen on cleanliness and usually bath twice daily.

The great temples are all accessible from the water and mostly have their main facade turned towards the river or a great canal. Special landing places and staircases into the water are always built for temple visitors. The Siamese carry out entire pilgrimages by boat. Bastian remarks (*Reisen in Siam*, page 57): "In the spot where the Menam flows into the sea, in the middle of the water besides a small isle, there is a temple, built on an artificial base, which is visited at certain times of the year by many pilgrims and which is venerated by circumnavigation with boats. During the races, which are held at the same time, the Siamese demonstrate an English passion for gambling (see Plate 11)." Usually the Siamese row standing in the back part of the boat. In the royal boats, however, the oarsmen sit with their face in the direction of navigation.

Population

In accordance with the three main parts of the country there are also three main parts of the population: in the Malay States the Malay, in Upper Siam the Lao or Thai Yai, in Lower Siam the southern Siamese or Thai Noi, who are the dominant class and from whom the bureaucratic nobility is constituted.

The negrito race, the remainders of which are living on inaccessible mountain areas of the Malay Peninsula, are assumed to be the original population. In prehistoric times the Indochinese Peninsula was settled from the South by Proto-Malay who live on as small peoples in enclosed valleys in Upper and Lower Siam. Then came the Mon and Khmer peoples. The latter are today still settled in Cambodia on the most distant borders of Southeast Siam. From 800 until about 1200 AD the Khmer Empire flourished in the Southeast of the country with Angkor as capital. The Peguans or Mon formerly constituted a great empire between Burma and Siam. It was however completely destroyed in the continual bloody wars between the two great neighboring countries. While the Mon were completely oppressed in Burma, a greater colony of them has settled south of Bangkok, near Paklat. There are about 50,000 of them, who speak their own language, possess their own Buddhist monasteries and who cultivate their own literature and also possess their own printing works.

Then the Thai tribes, who were pushed into the Indochinese Peninsula in constant fighting with the Chinese (from about 2000 BC), immigrated from the North into the country. First came the Thai Yai or the great Thai, the Lao, the present inhabitants of Upper Siam, who founded several flourishing kingdoms there which were united into one unit under King Phra Ruong I (about 1200 AD). As the last source of immigrating Thai tribes the Thai Noi or the small Thai came into the Peninsula just after 1300. Their fellow tribesmen let them pass without obstructing them. They founded the kingdom of Ayuthia around 1350, which soon exerted dominion over all Thai tribes and which also made Cambodia its suzerain. Until the year 1510 this Kingdom of Ayuthia included the whole Malay Peninsula; after this, some states, and in 1867 Cambodia, which ended up under French protectorate, were lost. In the Burmese wars the Province of Tenasserim in the North-West of the Malay Peninsuula was lost.

Today Siam is inhabited by about nine million people, of whom a little less than about one tenth are located in the capital of Bangkok with its close vicinity. The Lao (Thai Yai) and the southern Siamese (Thai Noi) together constitute about seven million people; the rest are Chinese, Malay, Peguans and Cambodians as well as ethnic minorities.

The Lao, the descendants of the earlier Thai Yai, live in Upper Siam. We distinguish the Lao Pung Kao and the Lao Pung Dam, i.e., the white and the black Lao. The former live in the vicinity of Luang Prabang and their territory is today for the greatest part a French colonial possession, while the Lao Pung Dam live in Chiangmai, Lampoon, Lampang, Phrae, Nan and Lakhon and formerly constituted their own principalities which had to pay tribute to the King of Siam. While the Lao live in the valleys and the plains of northern Siam, the higher mountains are inhabited by other small tribes. To these belong the Kho or Kha peoples, the Yao, the Meo, etc.

The Karen and the Karieng live on the mountain range situated along the Siamese-Burmese border. Shan tribes live in the North of the kingdom and on the mountains of the southeastern province of Chantabun. Besides these there are a host of populations, Siam's population tables showing very many names of the most varied tribes which for the greater part do not inhabit united territories.

In Indochina a custom existed formerly for the king to take away part of the population of a hostile country after its conquest as prisoners of war and settle them in various provinces, mostly of his own dominions. Thus we have all around the present capital of Bangkok small colonies of prisoners of war of tribes who constitute a living monument of the victorious military campaigns of the Siamese kings, besides being forced to provide the king certain services and levies. Prince Dilock (*Landwirtschaft in Siam*, page 16) says about them: "These people remained slaves of the king and form a separate part of the country's population. In case of war they are used as soldiers, even against their own king. They serve their new master with the same loyalty as their former. They felt entirely like his subjects and as if they were born in the country."

In the Middle Ages constant wars depopulated the Indochinese Peninsula. One of the bravest nations were the Siamese. Therefore they took a lot of prisoners of war among the neighboring peoples. Associated closely with this is that the population is a very mixed one. To this has to be added the peaceful immigration, especially of Chinese. Because the wages for labor are higher in Siam than in their home countries and profitable opportunities exist, Chinese of the poorer class are continually migrating to try their luck in Siam. Their numbers have reached one and a half million.

Character

The Siamese proudly call themselves Thai, i.e., the free. By nature they are kind-hearted but they have a great feeling for their nation and think they are the most important people on Earth. The centuries-old tradition of Buddhism has made them open-handed toward their fellow human beings. In the countryside where the bad influences of the great city and especially of the harbor city of Bangkok have not yet made themselves felt, they are carefree, cheerful and friendly, without guile or malice. However they have a certain inclination towards idleness; also the eagerness for games is very much developed among them and any kind of game is welcomed. During the time of the evening coolness at 5 p.m. one often sees five or six young people standing in a circle and playing among themselves with some kind of rattan ball using their feet, a game in which they display a very great skill. On the other hand, theater, music and dance shows are very much dedicated to Buddhism and are considered in their religion genuinely pious. They visit the temple, offer numerous gifts and give the priests their life necessities of rice and other supplements every day. Many Siamese, especially the inhabitants of the capital, look very hard-set. But if one speaks with them, they are polite and, especially towards higher ranking people, very obliging.

One must admire the great calm and resignation with which the higher-ranking Siamese approach every aspect of life. Even in the most difficult circumstances they do not lose their composure. Their diplomatic dexterity is very great and if in the latest times they have preserved their political independence, then it is for the greater part due to their state policy.

Characteristic for the Siamese character is the form of greeting. When two friends meet, the first question is "Is your health okay?" If this question is replied to affirmatively, the second is: "Do you have *sanuk*?" *Sanuk* is one of the most important words in the Siamese language and means joy, contentment and pleasure. The opposite of *sanuk* is *lambak*: trouble, annoyance, vexation. Now, among the Siamese, everything possibly, which we Europeans do not experience as such, is *lambak*, for example work which goes beyond a certain degree. *Lambak* is everything that is not entirely according to one's wishes, waiting at the road, failure to fulfil a wish. Those enduring it also make no efforts to hide their feelings and freely say that they consider this or that a great *lambak*, for example, a long road or the fulfillment of an order which does not suit them. In no language in the world are there so many similarly sounding words for unpleasantness and *lambak* than in theirs. They are always ready for joy and banter. In respect to ill fate and other evil things they are very resigned and let go any misfortune with a *mai pen arai* which means "never mind."

They are very attached to the king and the government. They have such a great reverence for the sovereign that they do not dare to speak his name.

In Siam there are no restaurants and hotels. One can crisscross the whole country and everywhere one is lodged by the country-folk and receives food and accommodation. The most generous in this are the inhabitants of the many monasteries.

The Siamese are disposed completely differently from us and it is very unfortunate that we have brought to them, together with our outward civilization, the struggle for life and all modern achievements with their compulsion to work and the curse of the capitalist economy. Their childish cheerfulness and lively character is entirely clouded by this. Prince Dilock's statements about the character of his fellow compatriots are very interesting (*Landwirtschaft in Siam*, page 108): "The Buddhist religion has an extraordinarily great, but unfavorable influence on the whole economic life in Siam. The philosophical attitude to life of this religion has completely stupefied the people. It offers resistance against any progress and against every development to a higher culture, against the increase of wants and the fulfillment of needs, against every attempt to create a better existence and to acquire wealth by a higher education, energetic and intensive trade and industry and by greater diligence in work, against every economic competition, etc. In this lies the main reason for the fact that in Siam the economy in general and agriculture are not on a higher level yet. The Buddhist religion is much stricter in Siam than in the neighboring states because almost every Siamese must, as we have already mentioned, today still enter the monastery for some time before he can think about founding his own family. For centuries it has reigned in Siam and children are educated in the Buddhist philosophy of life very early. Later when they have grown up, for the Siamese to act against their religion is simply contrary to their nature.

They consider a violation of its rules not only a great sin but also as contrary to nature.

"Therefore it is very difficult for the government to say: 'You must work harder. You must work to gain progress,' because it knows only too well that the people do not follow these orders but act according to the religious principles even when they have to act against the demands of the state. The common, orthodox Siamese cannot understand why he should work more than is necessary for the fulfillment of his simple needs and why he should compete with others since he would only harm his brother by this.

"The Buddhist teachings completely reject the pursuit of progress. Therefore one often hears from those who do not know the Siamese conditions that the people are slow and lazy. But the Siamese cannot, according to the precepts of their religion, compete with others and their religion orders that they support others in need and mutually support each other.

"It is also connected to religion that several professions, for example, butchery, is not practiced by any Siamese. Cattle-raising they do but a real Siamese does not kill an animal since it is prohibited to take the life of any being according to the teachings of Buddha. To kill the smallest animal is an equally great sin as murdering a human being.

"However, the Siamese of today also kill animals, but only small ones, for example, poultry, and only for their own use, never as a profession.

"It is considered a great sin to raise animals to later sell them as cattle for slaughter or to slaughter them by themselves. But to raise animals to use them later as draft animals or beasts of burden is allowed. This is the reason why cattle and sheep-raising in Siam is mostly in the hands of the Hindus, Singhalese or

Malay and the Chinese and Peguans engage in raising pigs. The real Siamese only practice horse and buffalo raising.

"Only in the most recent times, since Siam has entered into a more intense trade with the European states, these conditions have somewhat improved. Because the export prohibition has been lifted and the prices in the interior are continually increasing, the people are forced naturally to engage in other professions because they could otherwise no longer live.

"The Siamese gradually start to wake up from their sleeplike condition and now also engage in cattle and pig-raising. One is allowed to hope with confidence that the economic conditions will improve over time if we were allowed to draw a conclusion from the present progress."

There could be no better testimony to the carefree, peaceful character of the Siamese than the sharp criticism of a Siamese who has entirely made our fundamentals and our way of thinking his own in Europe. Surely, a state like Siam cannot, in the long run, close itself off to the economic influence of Europe; from this honest confession of a Siamese we see however in shocking clarity how in contrast with its concepts the old culture of a distinguished people breaks down upon contact with modern European civilization. Prince Dilock himself perished as a result of this internal duality. When he went home after completing his studies, he could not accustom himself to the state of affairs in his fatherland and he took his own life after a few years.

Family

Until recently there was no public records office. It was sufficient when two people loved each other and lived together to be seen publicly as man and wife. When there were still serfs it was Siamese law that a servant was freed from serfdom and was considered a wife of her master if she had a child by him.

The usual form of marrying is some kind of purchase of a wife. The young man, who tries to obtain a girl, makes a gift of money or objects of value bargained for earlier by relatives to the mother of his future wife. By this he obtains the right to marry the daughter. He can however not force his wife to stay with him. Even less does he have the right of disposal over her. On the contrary, in case of ill treatment she can leave her husband and return to her parents without the dowry having to be given back to the husband. Formerly, according to Siamese law, it was in certain cases prescribed that the dowry be paid back to the husband by the parents of the bride if the woman left the man without him having any blame and she did not return. Today however the dowry is returned in all cases by the parents-in-laws. If women feel that they are slighted or offended by their husband or if they have left him for some other reason, they are brought back to the house of the husband by old women in a friendly and kindly manner. The latter have made a special profession out of this work.

The most important form of marriage is when the king gives a Siamese, in order to honor him or to reward his services, a woman from the retinue of his consorts. When the prominent Siamese intends to conclude a marriage they sometimes request the king to select a wife for them in accordance with ancient customs.

In upper classes the marriage is sealed by a contract between both families. Both partners bring property into the marriage. Very often the bride is presented a piece of land by her parents and the bridegroom has the duty to build the common residence on this piece of land.

Among less well-off people the parents on both sides give equal sums of money to the young couple so that it can found a household with it. Among farmers it is mostly the custom that the married children do not stay in the parental house. They obtain or rent land in the neighborhood of the parental farm. Great value is placed on the fact that the young family settles in the neighborhood so that during harvest time they can help each other.

The formality of marriage is not enacted by a church ceremony but is a strictly private affair. Nevertheless, with every marriage they call the Buddhist and Brahmin priests so that the former bless the union by prayers and the latter bestow happiness on the newly united by sprinkling holy water and by powerful apothegms.

The Siamese have very simple customs. Marriages can at any time be dissolved without any blame to the married people. Without any difficulties from the government or the relatives they leave each other, after the children and the property have been divided in a friendly manner. To marry again is possible without any other formality. Although Siamese law provides for courts to dissolve marriages, this is used very rarely. It is sufficient for both married persons who want to divorce, to inform their parents and their family about their wish and mutually to write a divorce agreement in the presence of their parents. It also speaks for the dignified, peaceful character of the Siamese that such divorces usually happen without any reproach, quarrel or dispute. Good morals dictate that one does not settle such family dealings in public before a court.

Until recently it was the custom in Siam to marry more than one woman, but this was only the case among the high-ranking and the rich. In marriages between Europeans and Siamese women it is customary that the woman does obtain some kind of salary besides sustenance. The man is also compelled to offer according to his means jewelry and other valuables. This is considered an appreciation of her marital merits in respect to the husband. The Siamese woman usually marries not before 15 to 16 years of age. Even these are exceptions and in the countryside the girls are 17 to 20 years old when they marry.

The children are raised very lovingly and almost never by corporal punishment; they obtain more from them by love and kindness than by strict discipline. During the first years they run around completely naked; only the girls wear a silver fig leaf on a small chain. On the other hand they start smoking very early. On the streets of Bangkok one can see children who are dressed with nothing but a cigarette. The hair is shaved very short among the small ones with the exception of a round spot on the head where the hair is left to grow and tied up in a tuft. Usually the children have a garland of fresh flowers around this tuft which is tightened with an expensive gold hairpin.

When they are five to six years old the children go to the monastery school where they are educated in arithmetic, writing, reading and in Buddhist religion. In an uneven year—in the 11th, 13th or 15th—the child's hair tuft is cut during the tonsure ceremony. This celebration is somewhat equivalent to our Confirmation [in the Protestant Church] and must among the girls be held before the beginning of puberty. The tonsure feast is celebrated with great pomp. Among important families a special edifice in the shape of a *mondob*[4] is built on the land of the family. The children are adorned with expensive brocade cloth and with rich gold and brilliant jewelry and made up like royal princes. After a complicated ceremony and after ritual baths the child takes it's place on a throne in the middle of the festive edifice. A white cotton thread is placed around the hair tuft. The thread leads to an elevated platform on the side on which the invited Buddhist priests are seated and say Pali prayers with the thread in their hands. Brahmin priests also participate in the feast by sprinkling holy water. After the tonsure ceremony they let the hair grow. The girls marry after a few years and the boys are usually drafted into the military when they complete their 18th year. When they are free of this, they usually go into the monastery when they are 20 years old. It is an old custom that every Siamese, before he has reached maturity, will have belonged to the Buddhist monkshood for at least a year. In the monastery he acquires knowledge of religion and completes his education.

In some families it is the custom that the boys go into the monastery right after the tonsure ceremony, being dressed in yellow cloth. They are given to a priest as *nen*, i.e., temple pupils, who look after their education and for whom they do in gratitude all kinds of services such as carrying his bag and other luggage, cook tea for him and otherwise look after his well-being. After the general adoption of the monastery schools, which take the place of our primary schools, this practice has been abandoned generally. Today they do not take the education of young men in the monastery so seriously. There are already many Siamese who do not enter the monastery or only for a short time. However, formerly the one who had not completed his education as a monk in the monastery was considered a heretic. He was considered a blasphemer and ill bred; they did not expect him to be capable of running his own business and lawfully he was considered an underage child. Nobody wanted to give him his daughter as a wife. People avoided him and, if he owned land, at harvesting time he would find nobody who would help him to carry out the fieldwork. Thus he was unacceptable to the society of people.

After his stay of two to three years in the monastery the young Siamese left the monkshood to marry and found his own household.

In general, the women are more diligent than the men. Special appreciation is accorded to mothers and in their later years their wish and will is followed if it is at all possible. The grandmother, the so-called Yai, enjoys even more esteem.

Agriculture

In Siam only part of the soil has been covered with agricultural crops. The population can still grow very considerably before all the soil suitable for agriculture has been made profitable. Therefore, within a foreseeable time, Siam will remain a rich agrarian state as it is now. With the exception of the urban population the people usually engage in agriculture, more precisely in rice cropping. Bad harvests among these are very scarce and therefore the net yield is proportionally high.

Because the whole country is the king's property, according to ancient custom and old practice, every Siamese has the right to ask the king for as much land as he can work with his family. But the desired field must be without master. It cannot belong either to a common pasture or meadow. For the land given them, formerly, the Siamese had to give one quarter of the harvest to the king as compensation or tax. More recently many laws have been left idle and the compensation has been noticeably reduced. Today the taxes must be turned over in currency. In order to obtain a piece of land, a Siamese must report to the *ampoe*, i.e., the administrator of the district in which the desired piece of land is located. The latter then prepares an act in which the land is turned over to the new owner at first for a year. But he cannot yet work it during this time period. Furthermore, it is publicly announced that the piece of land was acquired by the new owner in order that the rightful owner, if the land already belonged to somebody else, could lodge a protest. If,

after 30 days, nobody has reported, then the official of the Agricultural Ministry prepares a deed on the final ownership. The land however remains the property of the king and the owner only has a right of use. He can however sell, rent out, inherit and also freely transfer the land to others by testament but he must return it immediately to the king or the state if it is needed for the construction of railway lines, canals or is otherwise needed in the common interest. The present owner is then indemnified for his care by having conferred a similar plot of land and by an amount of money.

If the tilling of the transferred plots of land has not started after the end of the third year then they are again returned to the king, who then can give them to somebody else. If a Siamese does not want to till his land or keep it, he reports the land plots transferred to him to the government and then he does not have to pay tax on them anymore.

With certain limitations Europeans can also obtain plots of land in Siam according to these basic rules.

In general the land and soil of Siam are so fertile that the Siamese farmers do not need to use intensive agriculture. The agricultural practices and farming implements are still very simple and in remote areas they plow exactly like centuries ago. The earth is only opened up in furrows with the plowshare a few centimeters deep. Dressing with manure is not practiced at all. Also, they grow the same crop on the fields year after year.

In order to ensure for the population the cheapest possible food, formerly there was a general export prohibition for rice. Only when a rice stock for three years had been stored in the country did they export rice and then only by the government which had a monopoly on the rice trade. As a consequence of this it was very difficult to entertain trade relations with European states and to conclude trade treaties in modern terms. Besides rice, such monopolies also existed for most other export products. Formerly, this export was done by the king who had the rice exported to neighboring countries, especially China, on state ships. In this matter King Mongkut introduced change in the year 1855 with a great reform which allowed continual rice export. The Siamese grumbled at first against this new rule and it took a few years before they had got used to the new conditions. However, it was shown that King Mongkut was right because since that year the agriculture in Siam has developed considerably. The surface of worked land has increased very much, the price for rice has surely gone up but with this also the possibilities for profit. Primarily though, the wealth of the country has steadily increased since this time.

By the law that states that a countryman can only ask for the land from the king which he himself with his family can work, the approximate size of the farms is fixed. Large land ownership is proportionally scarce in Siam; it is in effect only the case for the *phu dee*, i.e., for nobles. Formerly, because of polygamy, the nobility had very large families. Siamese concepts mean that included in all families are those of servants as well as serfs and their families. Because the nobles thus had at their disposition a great number of workers, it was understandable that in accordance with this law, they obtained a greater piece of land which was only right because they had to feed all their serfs and everybody who belonged to their families. Through the abolishment of serfdom and its feudal relations the nobility lacks the workers to work the great, inherited estates. Because of this they sell or rent out the land if it is especially expensive. In other cases they report the estates to the state again. It has to be specially noted that the monasteries can also take part in the land ownership. Such pieces of land the people offer as gifts to the monastery. In general this is the exception and these estates are only a very small percentage of the whole cultivated area. This cannot be compared at all with the spread of the Dead Hand [of the pest] in the Middle Ages in Europe.

The land measurement of the Siamese is the *rai*, which is about 1,600 square meters (1 German *Morgen* is about 2,500 square meters). The usual size of the farmsteads is about 80 to 100 *rai*. Greater farms up to 200 *rai* are only found in areas that are extremely well situated or do not give any special problems in cultivation. In poorer areas, where this is not the case, the size of the farmsteads drops to 30 to 40 *rai*. Larger estates are up to 10,000 *rai*, rarely more than this.

The value of the land depends on the possibilities for irrigation. Rice is a marsh plant and therefore the better varieties of rice must be grown in flooded fields. Since the Menam floods the whole plain every year and this flood takes place regularly in a specific season, the fields in this region are especially sought after and the population throngs together here.

Through a widespread system of canals the more distant land in the plain has also been made workable for crops.

The rice fields are usually sub-divided into square plots one *rai* in size. Every single one of these fields is surrounded with a 90-centimeter high earthen dike, which is destined to contain the water led onto the field. During more recent times, not all of the fields are surrounded with such walls. This is dropped especially for fields located in lower lying areas which are covered by water during the regular inundation in any case and thus it is used only for higher lying fields to gather the rain water on the fields. Through the building of canals it is possible to flood also higher lying fields which are surrounded by earthen walls. For this purpose the Siamese use very ingeniously constructed treadmills and hand-driven scoops.

Several types of rice growing have developed, according to the water that is available. If a lot of water is available, first a small field is prepared as a plant nursery. The water must cover this part of the field with, if possible, an equal height of water of about 20 centimeters. Then the field is grazed, plowed and harrowed to remove all the weeds. Most often the plows are made of a single piece of wood, the forked branch of a tree. The proportionally small iron plowshare is triangular and has two sharp edges. It is pushed from the top through the wood so that it sticks out five centimeters at the bottom. This less than perfect way of plowing produces small clods of earth and the soil is not turned over but only opened up. As beasts of burden they use water buffaloes with wide open, large horns (see Plate 58). They are most suitable for these wet marshy fields because they have such a thick skin they do not have to fear the leeches. The farmers steer the animals only by shouting to them not by the bridle and they know exactly into which direction they have to go. The square harrow is produced entirely from bamboo wood. Because it is very light the farmer stands on it while using it. Horses are not used in Siamese agriculture, oxen only exceptionally if the soil is very dry and there is no fear for leeches. The rice seeds are left for two days in the water

and germinate for three days. Then they are sown thickly in the nursery beds; the young rice shoots grow very quickly so that after two to three weeks they are half a meter high already. Then they are taken from the wet soil and transplanted in the fields which must be covered everywhere with water. About five to ten shoots are planted together at distances of 20 to 30 centimeters (see Plate 59). In order for the rice to grow well the water in the fields must be at least 25 centimeters high but cannot be higher than 2.5 to 3 meters. With the heightening inundation the rice plants grow.

After about four months the fields are ready to be harvested. They cut off the rice plants with a sickle. Our scythes would cause too much loss of grains because of shaking during the mowing. If the inundation has passed, they cut the rice at waist height and tie it up in sheaves. They are brought together in great heaps. If the water has not subsided sufficiently, they harvest from a boat. In this method only the ears are cut and loaded onto the boat immediately. They are hung up from special racks to dry. For a threshing-floor a very flat piece of soil is found which is made especially smooth and more compact still. It is covered it with thinned cow dung and in this way hinders dust production. In the middle of the threshing-floor a post is erected. Around it the ears are placed in layers. The grain is removed by the treading of the buffalo, which is chased around the post. The greatest number of buffaloes used is about ten. They are all tied together in a row. The buffalo at the outside right wing is tied to the central post of the threshing-floor with a leather strap. A boy chases the animals around by grabbing the outside most buffalo by its tail and leading it. The grains are then collected, stacked in flat, large baskets and the husks and other mixed-up matter removed by throwing the grain into the air and catching it again with the baskets. The wind then blows away husks and empty ears. In poorer areas where the people have insufficient buffaloes for the treading, they still thresh with the flail. They wait with threshing and treading until after the high waters. If the rice stocks are so depleted that they need new grain before the ending of the high waters, they thresh in the house by hitting several rice sheaves together against a sieve of bamboo sticks. The grains then fall through the very wide meshes of the sieve.

The rice grains are usually hulled in a great wooden mortar, which has been produced from a tree trunk, with a hand-operated pestle or also with a foot pestle as is shown in Plate 37. The hulling of the rice is mostly done by young girls. In Lower Siam hand mills are used. Today the rice is mostly hulled in steam mills in which the rice grains are polished, i.e., the glassy skin under the husk is removed. Formerly, by the continual use of polished rice the feared beriberi illness had erupted in the Siamese army and navy. Because rice is the main staple food of the Siamese for them, rice hulled by hand in a wooden mortar is much more wholesome. As has been shown by medical science, the glass skin of the rice contains important vitamins.

Upper Siam is mostly a mountainous country. The populations of Karen, Karieng and other hill tribes, who change their house locations every year and who could be considered semi-nomadic people, do not possess flooded rice fields. They can only grow rice varieties that do well on dry soil. Because the fertilization by the mud of the Menam is lacking they are forced to leave the harvested fields in the following year and find new ones. The old soil needs a few years rest to be conducive to a harvest again. Thus, these populations only return after three to four years to their former fields. In order that no difficulties arise, every tribe has its own region in which the tribesmen can settle freely. These areas are very large because the mountains in Upper Siam are very thinly populated.

In this kind of rice-cropping the land is first reclaimed, the fields which they want to use are deforested in January and the wood is left until the beginning of April to dry in the sun and then they burn it. The ashes are used as fertilizer for the soil. The hill tribe people do not need harrows or plows to prepare the land. They lay two bamboo sticks on the ground, a man walks along these with a sharp stick in each hand and he stabs 3 to 4 centimeter deep holes in the soil, for which the bamboo stick is used as a guide. The holes are thus arranged more or less in a straight row. His wife walks with a basket of rice grains behind him, throws 8 to 10 grains in every hole and then closes it with her foot. As soon as the rainy season starts, the rice germinates and shoots up. The mountain people do not bother with their fields until the harvest. Other kinds of grain such as wheat, maize, barley and oats are also grown but in smaller quantities.

In South Siam, especially in the vicinity of Bangkok, horticulture is widespread. For this the land areas are crisscrossed by a canal system. Every single field is surrounded by a one-meter high earthen wall. The field itself is then still traversed by several parallel water trenches. Mostly fruit trees are planted such as banana, breadfruit, durian, mango, orange, papaya, mangosteen, as well as coconut, sugar, areca, date and sago palms. Siam is rich in many other fruit varieties. They also cultivate with great results: the most varied pepper varieties, tobacco, indigo, cardamom, clove, nutmeg, sesame, hemp, cotton, coffee, cumin, ginger, saffron, vanilla, sugar cane, tea, groundnut, poppy and many other spices and trade crops. As vegetables the following must be noted: beans, peas, cauliflower, garlic, melons, pumpkins, cucumber, cabbage, lettuce, celery, garden radish, turnip, mustard seed and tomato. However the farmers of Siam have steadily turned more to rice cropping and abandon at present the cultivation of spices, trade crops and vegetables because rice culture is more profitable and allows in some areas even three harvests per year.

Because of the luxuriance of the tropical vegetation in Siam so far no cattle fodder has been grown on fields. The state still has sufficient idle land which it lets the people use freely as meadows and pastures. Because eternal summer reigns in Siam, the cattle have sufficient food throughout the entire year. Haymaking in the strict sense is not practiced; the meadows are only grazed by the animals. After the harvest the cattle is chased into the fields to graze the stubble. No limitations are placed in its way: the cattle can walk about anywhere. The farmers mutually allow each other general grazing rights.

Because of religious reasons cattle raising is not widespread among the Siamese. The true Siamese almost never engage in it contrary to the Malay, Mon, Chinese and the hill tribes. As draft animals for plows and carts the Siamese catch water buffaloes and bulls in the forests, especially in the vicinity of Korat. The method to catch them is very simple. At the edge of the forest the farmers dig a row of pits one after the other. They surround a buffalo herd in the forest and chase them towards the pits into which the buffaloes fall. The animals caught are tied and brought into the stables.

The hill tribes from the North wander with their herds like nomads throughout the country and sell the farmers the draft animals they need. Because during recent times the price for animals has gone up considerably, the farmers are starting to engage themselves in breeding them; they do not, however, sell the animals for slaughtering.

Especially important for Siamese agriculture are the water buffaloes, which perform best on the marshy wet soil of the rice fields. They can work all day long in the water. After the time for working they lie about in a muddy puddle which serves as their night shelter. The wet mud cools them during the hot time of the day and protects them against vermin.

The Siamese do not engage in the dairy industry because the smell and taste of milk, butter and cheese upsets them; Siamese cows also produce little low-fat milk.

The farmers draw great profits from bee keeping, but bee keeping as such is still unknown. The wild bees are chased from their beehives with smoke. Bees wax is in high demand for candles that are used as temple gifts.

Civil Relations

The relations between the various classes in Siam are so peculiar and so different from other peoples that they must be especially emphasized.

In principle, the entire surface of the kingdom belongs to the king. He is the unbounded master and distributes the land plots to his subjects. If the state system is that of an absolute monarchy, the kings have reigned benevolently, especially the one of the present dynasty.

The king stands facing the people who are divided in *phu dee* or nobles and in *phrai* or commoners. To the *phu dee* belong as the first class the princes of the royal house, then come the sovereigns of the vassal states and finally the *kha raja kan*, the officials who are sub-divided into the nobles of the right and of the left hand. Because the king on his throne looks East those on his right hand side stand in the South and they are called *kha raja kan wai thahan* (military nobility). The *kha raja kan pholaruen* (civil officials) stand on the left side or in the North.

Until recently hereditary nobility was un-known in Siam. There were old families who strictly maintained their traditions and who held for many generations high positions in state service, for example, the Suriwong family, who maintained their own great family temple, Vat Phra Juravong (i.e., literally: temple of the prominent family). Most recently the present king has conferred hereditary noble ranks on such families only, which have nothing to do, however, with the civil service nobility and rank alongside it. The nobility of the *kha raja kan* (i.e. literally: servants of the royal work) is only a service nobility, conferred at the same time as the civil service position. It is also only personal. The steps of it are starting from below: *Mün*,[5] *Khun, Luang, Phra, Phya, Chao Phya*, after this, formerly, also *Somdet Chao Phya*. The last title is no longer conferred today.

The ranks are not sharply separated one from the other and the Indian caste system is unknown. Every Siamese can be elevated to the highest rank if he possesses the necessary abilities. Thus, during my stay in Siam, the under-secretary of state of the interior, Phya Maha Ammat, who later rose to the function of minister of the interior and, above this, to viceroy in the provinces, was in his youth a simple servant but by intelligence and special skills he had worked himself up to this position. On the other hand, all the members of the numerous royal families also strive to be employed in state service and to rise further. Also, princes can still rise higher through the conferment of titles. Because in Siam the rewarding of any merit depends on the king, completely different from European states, all are striving to distinguish themselves in his eyes.

While on the one hand the service nobility is personal, on the other the ranks which the princes of the royal house take, are also only personal. Until most recently polygamy was the custom in Siam. As a consequence of this, one differentiates among the princes between those who descend from the women of the same rank as the king, thus princesses, and those who are born from secondary wives. The former bear the title *Chao Fa*, i.e., heavenly princes. The different ranks of princes are in order *Kromamün, Kromakhun, Kromaluang, Kromaphra, Kromaphya*—thus the same titles and the same rank order as among the civil service nobility but with the prefix *krom*. The son of a prince only bears the title *Mom Chao*; the Son of a *Mom Chao* is a *Mom Rajawong* and his son is once more a man of the common people,[6] who only bears the tile *Nai*, which is exactly the same as our designation Mister. Only free people can bear this title while criminals and convicts are addressed with *ai*.

It is a peculiarity of the Siamese service nobility that the title which the civil servant in question retains is at the same time also linked with a special name, which characterizes in particular the service of the official. With this title he is also addressed and his own civilian name recedes entirely into the background. If an official dies, his title and name are free and the king confers both on another civil servant. Because in the history books of Siam private names are never used, everything personal disappears behind the government title. In later times, one cannot know which personality hid behind this. Individuality is so far, in this absolutely governed state, only allowed the king. The idea of him retaining complete power has nowhere been followed through more consequently. In the end, all officials of he country owe rank, status and wealth to the king who can, as pleases him, elevate and downgrade them. The dependency relationship is therefore a much stronger one than in any other monarchic state. This is also expressed in the court ceremonial of which we will speak below.

The southern Siamese have conquered the whole kingdom militarily. Therefore, they are the dominant section of the population and are favored generally in the assignment of the positions for officials. There are also officials from other populations but their numbers are small. The civil servants are very highly regarded among the people. The Siamese are therefore very eager to obtain such a post.

The common people or *phrai* were formerly sub-divided into two groups: in the free Thai and the dependent *that*. In European sources the dependents [or serfs] have always been designated slaves but this is completely misleading. Seldom has the relationship between masters and serfs been so lenient as in Siam. By the great reforms of King Chulalongkorn this relationship of serfdom has been abolished, not suddenly but gradually. There still may be isolated serfs but none under 56 years of age. With the shorter average lifetime of the Siamese this is quite a relatively high age. In a few years the serfs will have died out. The decisive reforms came after the return of King Chulalongkorn from his first European journey in 1897.

The strange serfdom system of the Siamese however deserves a short consideration. Apart from the lack of freedom of the prisoners of war, the serfdom was a remarkable system of indebtedness. Siamese who could not in these expensive times feed their families themselves, obtained from a well-to-do gentleman an amount of debt. Officials drew up an agreement about this. The debtor hired himself out to the creditor for personal services until the repayment of the debt. He always had the right to pay back this amount and thus to buy back his freedom. If he had family they too came into the dependency relationship with the creditor. The serfs had to perform personal services in the house or on the land of the master. For this the master had to supply them food, housing and clothes. The work done was considered the interest for the capital received which was not reduced by the labor done. Only by the repayment of the loaned amount could the debtor become free again. The children, who were born during the time of the service relationship were also serfs and thus liable to serve. However, they could be set free by payment and an elaborate legal framework exists about the amounts of the repayment at various ages and for each sex. Prince Dilock (*Landwirtschaft in Siam*, page 34) remarks about this: "Everybody was free to pay back the loaned capital to hire himself out to another master or to return to his earlier free state. The master did not have the right, during his lifetime, to turn over the debtors in his service against their will to another person by sale or loan. By testament this was however allowed. The master was forced to receive the money if it was paid back. [...] Free parents could also sell their children as debt-slaves. [...] The reasons for debt-slavery of free men were usually the emergencies of the concerned, which however are not only caused by the poor business of a company, misfortunes, etc., but often also brought about—especially among the farming population—because of the age-old and in recent times, i.e., the time of the immigration of many Chinese to Siam, alas extremely widespread, passionate gambling among the Siamese. After harvesting times, as is the case today, great feasts took place according to old customs and traditions in which they also gambled and the farmers often lost not only their currency but also their house and farmstead and all their possessions. Also, when farmers went on ships and boats with their grain to Bangkok and other great towns to sell it, after the sale they often went into the gambling houses and when they had lost the proceeds from their grain, and being without cash, they took a loan against a promise of debt serfdom. Sometimes they also immediately lost this loan in the gambling houses and accumulated more debt by a new loan, which they could no longer pay with their house and farmstead. Uncountable Siamese have become debt slaves through gambling."

Because serfdom in Siam showed itself in such a lenient form, the population was so used to this dependency that often it could not go along with the position created by the new law. Until the World War there were many former serfs who lived with their masters as before and indeed, continued to live in the old dependency relationships although they had been freed a long time ago according to the law. With the freedom of work, they could not get used any more to the struggle for life without protection and support. Above freedom they preferred serfdom which offered them an assured, although dependent, existence. It happened often when the law became effective that the serfs begged their masters to keep them and to give them the livelihood and protection which they had formerly received from them and indeed the masters also granted the requests of old servants, although this caused them a lot of trouble. One can observe here also the influence of the teaching of Buddha, to be merciful for all forms of life.

At the time of a failed harvest in the province of Chantabun Siamese came to me in my house and wanted to sell me their little seven-year old girl as a serf, although this has for long not been allowed by law. The population cannot free itself immediately from the customs which have existed for many centuries perhaps even thousands of years, and the old relationship continues to exist in their feelings as before.

Until the year 1897 the law of 1592 about the redeeming of serfs was still in effect. The personal relationship between master and dependents was in general good and patriarchal with the best treatment of the dependent. There is also splendid evidence about this in the writing of French Jesuits who were in Siam in the second half of the seventeenth century. The French bishop Pallegoix and the English diplomat Bowring report likewise in the middle of the previous century.[7]

Feudal Rights

Until recently Siam was a medieval feudal state with completely developed feudal laws. Although this feudal right has been abolished by law for a few decades, today it still exerts influence and knowledge of the old relationships is generally necessary to understand present-day Siam.

We have already written above that the serfs were subject to a master. Also free people had to select a patron. These patrons were subject to a master and the latter was again under a higher one; thus it went upwards to the princes of the royal house, who were then under the king. In this way the whole people was liege to the king. In this duty of liege the primary factor was that the individual Siamese were doing personal work for the king. Exempted from this were priests, women and children only. When reaching the 18th year of age the young men were presented for inscription in the drafting lists by their patrons or, in the absence of the latter, their fathers. At this time, the concerned men were tattooed on their left hands with a mark, which was different according to their professions. The whole population was sub-divided into guilds. According to an age-old right and law the son of a blacksmith became a blacksmith himself and he could only exercise the profession of his forefathers. All the guilds were sub-divided into feudal people of the right and of the left hand as we saw among the officials, according to the Indian example. One distinguishes the *tahan* class (soldiers) and the *polarüen* (craftsmen). However several guilds which, according to our view, belong to the craftsmen, belonged to the soldier class, for example, carpenters. Right and left is conceived with the person of the king as origin. When the king is seated on the throne, he looks East; thus right is for him South and left North. The soldier class is thought to be standing on the right, while the craftsmen belong on the left side. [...] It should be specified here that the planet Mars dominates the South, thus appropriately the soldiers are standing also in this direction.

The duty to work lasts until the 60th year. Exempted from personal work for the king, except old people, were only those who prevented from working by bodily infirmities. All members of the *phu dee* class, i.e. the nobility, were exempted from the tattooing. Their services to the government, which they delivered uninterruptedly, freed them from the work for the king. The time of service in any year was different for each guild. Furthermore, this underwent several changes in the course of the centuries. In any case it was possible to free oneself from this personal service duty by the payment of a proportionately small amount of money. In the 17th century de la Loubère reported that they lasted six months annually. In the 18th century four months annually were fixed and in the 19th century, especially during the last quarter century, this time was further reduced. Since 1900, in the place of personal service duty, a poll tax has been introduced generally but it is not the same for the whole kingdom, is set low for poor regions and in many areas it is completely dropped. In case of failed harvests the people even receive monetary support from the king.

Formerly, the patron also had the duty to protect his clients in lawsuits. If things went well for the patron and he was honored by the king, then his clients also took part in the elevation to a higher rank and all the honor which the patron experienced was also counted as his share by the client. To feasts which the patrons organized the clients had to contribute according to their wealth and of course they were also guests. Even after the abolishing of feudal rights these relationships still continue to exert influence, for example when in the Ministry of Public Works the 80th birthday of the minister's mother was celebrated many, even the European officials, had to contribute ten percent of their monthly salary to hold the celebrations.

The patron was responsible for assuring that the clients performed the prescribed personal labor for the king every year. If he had 100 clients, then he could let 10 to 20 of them work for himself as a compensation for his supervision. If his clients bought themselves free from the personal labor, then he held 10 to 20 per cent of this money for himself. Today men are no longer forced to work for their patrons. However, since a soldier usually has great estates, he would not be able today to work the whole area any more if his former clients would not work freely on their cultivation. in exchange. He supports them again in all legal and tax matters against the state. The old relationships thus continue to exist, although weakened, in the modern state.

Jurisprudence

The laws of the Siamese were always very lenient. If the proof of guilt or innocence could not be established, the law allowed that the accused could absolve himself through a trial by ordeal. It consisted in the parties, both plaintiff and accused, diving into the water and holding themselves down by bamboo sticks. The one who could stay under water longest received the benefit of the law. Also the accused had to eat a rice ball over which special curses had been pronounced and which would, in case he had taken it while being guilty, explode his body. Sometimes the plaintiff and the accused were given two equally large rice balls to eat and the one who could eat it first without swallowing the wrong way won the case. But also more serious tests were demanded for example sticking a hand into boiling oil, or molten tin, or walking on glowing irons.

Today Siam has a modern legal jurisprudence. The death penalty is pronounced but its execution is practiced with leniency like before.

In the northern provinces a lawyer had got rid of a Buddhist priest, who had laid hands on his wife, by assassination. At first he had been acquitted by the local court; however the king who was introduced to the case sent him back to the regular courts with the argument that the instigator as much as the perpetrator had to be punished. In a second procedure the lawyer was condemned to death. When the conviction was confirmed by the king, the date for the execution was fixed. In the early morning he was first taken from the prison and brought in a festive parade to the monastery to which the murdered monk belonged. There a reconciliation feast was held and after the chief monk had pronounced the pardon, the procession moved towards the execution area. The official read the condemned man the death verdict, and the latter had the king's signature shown to him and did not show the least fear of death. The Siamese do not take death as tragically as Europeans do because they believe in reincarnation. A short pole, to which he would be tied, had been driven in the ground. Behind it the grave was dug. He sat down quietly, stood up once more because he was not sitting comfortably and did not let them tie his hands to the pole but waited calmly for the deadly blow. The two executioners, dressed in fire red colors, came nearer, kneeled before him, greeted him with their hands lifted up and explained to him that they had to kill him by force of the law and that he should not reproach them for this act. After they had obtained from his side the assurance that this should take place they sat facing him, handed him an opium cigarette and lit an ordinary one themselves. Through this dose of opium, the condemned entered a state of dreams. The executioners came closer to him, closed off his ears with wax without him noticing this and marked the spot on his neck where they had to hit him. Then they both performed a ceremonial dance behind his back in which they moved against each other and brandished great swords, which were glittering like flames in the sun, above their heads. The dance became more and more animated and faster and with one blow the first executioner had, after a short turn, separated the head of the condemned from his rump. The head was only hanging from a small fold of skin, which is considered a masterstroke of Siamese swordmanship. If the first executioner had missed, the second would have stepped in his place. During the whole ceremony the execution area was surrounded by military men who faced the spectators with loaded guns. Formerly it has happened that the family of the condemned made an attempt to free him at the last moment.

Cremation

It is a general custom in Siam, in accordance with Buddhist rites, to cremate the dead. Excepted from this are only the bodies of pregnant women, those who die during childbirth, small children who are stillborn or who die before they have teeth and, in addition, all people who die of seriously contagious diseases. They also do not hold executed criminals worthy of cremation. Most of these are dug up after three years at the latest and then cremated. Exempted from this are criminals and small children.

If a Siamese has died and the loud laments of the next of kin have stopped, the deceased is washed and wrapped in ribbons of white cloth. They put the body in a coffin, which has four side walls and a cover, but instead of a bottom there is an iron grill on which the body is placed. Among the common Siamese the body is burned after a few days. While the deceased has been placed on a bier, the relatives ask the priests to come. They take their place on elevated seats placed along the wall behind the coffin on elevated seats and read holy Pali prayers from palm-leaf books or from the book "The Travels of Priest Phra Malai to Heaven and Hell." Then they are offered yellow cloths or money. Every Siamese feels closer to one temple or the other, because the temple has been entirely or partly founded by that family or because, by rich gifts offered the temple, there exists an especially good relationship with their priests. Almost every Siamese especially favors a special temple with his gifts by erecting, according to his means, a great or a small Buddha statue or honors the *phra chedi* and religious edifices in it by hanging it with cloths or scarves.

Once the selection of a cremation site been completed, for which they prefer mostly the yard of a monastery, and everything is ready for the cremation, then a hole is broken in the house wall. The friends and relatives gather and the body is removed through this hole from the house and carried three times around it.[8] Then the whole mourning procession goes in white clothes to the cremation site.[9] All men who are younger than the deceased have their head hair shaved. Only the elders and those who have a higher rank than the dead wear a black *pha nung* and a white overcoat. At the cremation site the coffin is placed on the funeral pyre, the cover is removed, the priests say their recitations and commence the prayers of the pall. Then they sprinkle the face of the deceased with coconut milk and light the fire. The friends and relatives place sandalwood on the pyre. The coffin is protected from burning by pouring water on it. The fire is maintained as long as it takes for the whole body to turn to ashes, which takes about two hours. Then the fire is extinguished, the ashes and remains of bones are collected and placed in a wooden or porcelain urn. Usually the latter is interred into the foot of a *phra chedi*. More recently these ash-urns have been placed in the bell towers of *phra chedi*, but the Buddhist priests react strongly against this in their preaching, because this honor is reserved for true Buddhist relics. To circumvent this prohibition they place a small Buddha relic or a small Buddha statuette on the ashes. If the family does not dispose of sufficient money to erect a sepulchral edifice then the urn with the ashes is placed on the altar of a temple in front of the Buddha statue, or at home on the altar of the house Buddha statue.

For prominent Siamese the body is first embalmed because the preparations for the cremation take a long time. They cover the body with fragrant spices, incense, myrrh, honey and pour mercury into the mouth to protect the intestines from decomposition. The body is then wrapped all around very tightly with narrow ribbons of white cloth while spices are added continuously; only the head is left free, otherwise it looks similar to an Egyptian mummy. Because of the long time it lies in waiting the body dries out more and more until in the end it is only bones and skin. In many cases such bodies have remained in waiting for several years, even in the tropical climate, without any kind of decomposition occurring. Captain Werner, who stayed with the Prussian Expedition of 1861 in Bangkok, describes a cremation as follows: "In one of our walkabouts we ended on the cemetery grounds and had the opportunity to see the burning of a body. It was the wife of a prominent Siamese and therefore the celebrations were accompanied by great pomp. The place is in the middle of the city on the left bank of the river, is very large, covered with lawns and here and there planted with trees. It has the shape of a half-circle of which the periphery is constituted by a wall and the chord builds a street of the city. Around the middle of the circumference a small temple-like edifice rises up. It rests on an eight to ten feet high square base, is square itself and opens on all four sides in order that one can see the entire insides from all over the courtyard. In the middle of this temple there is a fireplace and from the ceiling hangs on chains a coffin-like box of sheet-iron with a bottom woven with strong wire. In this box is placed the body brought to the place in a wooden coffin and then, underneath, with strongly fragrant resinous wood, they make a great fire in which the officiating priests pour a fragrant oil from time to time. In half an hours time the procedure is completed which in general does not produce an unpleasant but rather a festive impression because one can only see the flames and priests silently poking the fire. If the Lord Buddha has ordered the burning of bodies based on whichever religious reason, he certainly has provided a great service to the public health service. All the noxious fumes which so often in great cities emanate from the cemeteries to spoil the air and which become very dangerous more easily in a hot climate have been prevented by this procedure.

"An open hall has been built in a half-circle around the temple. Under it the relatives and the mourners, dressed in white mourning dress like in China and Japan, attend the ceremony. There also are seated, according to the payment, a greater or smaller number of priests who chant funeral chants with in front of their faces a palm fan and, finally, there is a group of musicians squatting on the ground in order to glorify the festive mood with the tones of their instruments. Thousands of curious spectators fill the courtyard and the whole scene would leave an august impression if it would not end quite regularly in a scuffle which little suits the earnestness of the subject. Namely, when the body has been burned, the closest relatives distribute money among the people by throwing it to the crowd from two specially built balconies. Now, because the Siamese coins are not like ours flat but round and the smallest are barely the size of peas, they are placed in oranges which are then thrown down."

Among prominent families, especially the bodies of the royal houses and higher-ranking notables who are close to the king, the bodies are preserved for several months, even for a year or longer according to the rank of the deceased. The body is placed on a bier on an elevated platform; royal bodies are placed in a kneeling upright position in gold urns inside a splendid edifice, especially built for the purpose in the city palace. Almost daily Buddhist monks hold funeral chants at the body. Funeral music and lamentations by especially hired mourning women are held. During this period they built on the cremation site—for which in the case of royalty bodies an open field situated north of the main palace, the *phra men* grounds, has been reserved— several edifices for the cremation. In the middle stands a high building crowned at the top with a splendid canopy in which the funeral pyre is stacked up. In addition there are platforms for mask and marionette games, Chinese comedies and the equipment to produce fireworks. They also erect posts for rope-dancers and magicians. In addition they plan for lantern dances and stage plays. Many buildings are adorned with spendthrift splendor and richly covered with gold decorations. The exterior shapes are very similar to the temple architecture of Siam. When all the ceremonial umbrellas and the preparations have been completed then the funeral urn is brought in a great funeral procession to the cremation site. Usually the main part of the procession is constituted by four large, royal carriages completely covered with gold which are crowned in their middle part by a mostly splendid baldachin. In the first the praying monks are seated; in the second are young royal children of about 14 years of age who scatter flowers; the third carriage supports the urn and the fourth is loaded with sandalwood for the funeral pyre. Formerly, images of fantastic animals, which

were filled with gifts for the priests, then followed. The whole train moves slowly to the lamenting melody of a sad funeral march. After the urn has been placed on the funeral pyre by several ceremonies, the monks say the pall prayers and others which deal with the ephemeral character of all earthly existences. Then they direct the full powers of their minds on the mysterious holy Nirvana. After the pious chants the priests are handed the four kinds of gifts, new cloths, gift platters and similar such things. During this time the mask, marionette and shadow-play theaters perform, Peguan dancers are dancing and Chinese theater-players and dancers from Tavoy play. In front of the funeral pyre these games are held for three, five, seven or nine days. Bastian, who witnessed such a cremation at the court of the King of Siam in 1862, presents the following report about it:

"In May, one of these festive cremations took place for a son of the king, who had died nine months ago. For this purpose the whole courtyard between the palaces of the first and second kings had been changed into a city of tents with an indescribable multitude of decorated temples, brightly colored pleasure-castles, towers bedecked with flags, halls bending under ornaments, pagodas, kiosks, and pavilions. Witnesses colored like walls hide the bamboo frames of the interiors. The entire road to here was already covered with theater stages on which, partly, Chinese family dramas are staged, and partly, in the grotesque manner of dramatized epics heroes held their armor dances in glittering outfits together with giants and monsters. They also danced in the way of the Mon or Peguans, i.e., in ordinary clothes. An avenue with cone-shaped pagodas leads to the entrance of the main building in the middle column hall of which the sarco-phagus was placed. It jutted out with richly decorated terraces and carried on its top under a cone-shaped roof the urn with the body (*borommakot*), in front of which a figure in royal dress kneeled down. In front of the sarcophagus the Brahmins were seated; to the right several princes and to the left a thick curtain shielded the royal throne. Furthermore, there are two separate rooms furbished for the king and inaccessible for the public. One of the former leads to the gift room in which four rows of monks dressed in new habits were seated with in front of them the offerings (gift bowls, cloths, fans, cushions, platters, etc.). The king who entered surrounded by his small children was wearing a white scarf on top of his black costume and some of the princes wore dark, but besides them all the mourners of the royal family were dressed in white which is the color of mourning in Siam. The king took a few of the displayed toys to distribute them to his children. Then he lit a few candles and handed them as a sign of his reverence to the holy men. Then the eldest daughter of the deceased came closer on her knees and pushed a few boxes of gifts in front of her until she had reached the seat of the monks for whom these were destined. In order to more quickly distribute the gifts among the priests a host of small boys, partly sons of the king with head tufts and partly the sons of the deceased who had their heads shaved because of the event of the demise, came to help. After the king had them bring a few baskets with lotus flowers and some others with lotus seeds, the priests started a recitative hymn, while their faces were hidden behind the upright standing fans. Next to the central building there was a similar smaller one in which the urn with the body had to be brought for the cremation. All doors were guarded by monster-like giant figures and umbrellas with seven layers (made of gold and silver witnesses) were standing around. In one part of the pleasure grounds there were artificial rocks with holes and caves or small ponds with *papier mâché* houses and puppets inside. The soldiers had dressed up in uniforms as did the orchestras, but the guards in the immediate vicinity of the king were bearing lances. Some of the servants dressed in the white morning color were bearing richly decorated swords on their sides.

In several places restaurants, which held open tables at the expense of the sovereign or of prominent persons for their acquaintances, had been set up.

When we went there again the next day, the urn had already been brought into the cremation tower. The king sent a tea platter with lottery tickets, i.e. fruit peels glued together which, when opened, had a paper inside with the number of the object won. One of my prizes was a betel box adorned with worked-in flowers, another a basket, a third a towel, I believe so at least. A beloved pleasure of the king at such festivities consists in throwing small gold coins among the skirmishing people, or to distribute to his friends lemons which contain silver or gold *ticals*. However, this time he was in a sad mood because in the morning of the same day his favored daughter, whom was closest to his heart, had contracted cholera. After a few hours she succumbed already and even before the funeral festivities had come to an end here, in the palace the lament for a new body already resounded.

When evening fell candles and incense sticks were distributed among the friends of the deceased. The king then came down to the platform on which the urn filled with inflammable materials was standing and lit it as the instruments started to play the music. When the king had retired, the whole retinue of relatives and friends followed in a queue to pass the body and to add their burning lights to the funeral pyre.

The flames licked through the iron grill, which surrounded the urn, and a thick smoke went up from the incense and sandalwood stacked there. After the relatives and prominent friends had fulfilled their last duty the whole household of the deceased prince, his employees, his servants and slaves, were allowed in. All with their heads shaved and dressed in white. Then came a long procession of women dressed in white cloth, also with shaved heads. They were the wives of the deceased as well as their companions and slaves and with only half suppressed sobs and sighing, with eyes red of weeping, they pushed forwards through the crowd of spectators to enter a room situated behind the catafalque from which soon escaped a heart-rendering moaning and lamenting. When we left the cremation site to return home, I saw standing at the exit door a woman weak from old age, with a shaved head and white clothes like the other mourners. She was weeping very bitterly—an image of deeply felt misery—and with one hand covered her face while, on the other, she held a lovely child that looked up asking and half-smiling to her with its clear and pretty eyes because in its innocence it did not understand the pain which its grandmother, so near her grave, perhaps expressed in tears for her, because her last and only protector had passed away."[10]

Court Life and Festivities

At the beginning of the Ramakien, the Siamese version of the Indian Ramayana, it is reported that the god Phra Narai (Vishnu) changed himself into a boar in order to vanquish the frightful giant Hirantayak who wanted to destroy the entire globe. After this victory the god returned to his snake throne in the West of the great sea of the world. He fell asleep there. While he was sleeping a splendid lotus flower sprang from his navel. When it opened, it contained a fine lad. Vishnu woke up, was very happy with the boy, took him on his arm and brought him to the highest god, Sayompuvanat (Shiva). The latter adopted him as his offspring and decided that he would be the first king on Earth. He immediately had called the god Phra In (Indra), the king of the Davadung Heaven, and ordered him to go down to Earth with his holy multitudes and to build there a splendid city for the future king. Phra In flew to Earth with a great following. First came a troop of gods who carried peacock tails in their hands, then a second with lion's manes, a third with dragon claws, and then a fourth with the stalks of lotus flowers. Then Phra In himself came. He was riding on his elephant Eirawan, with its 33 heads, which was delightful to see. On each head of the elephant a golden throne heaven rose up. At each of these there was a lotus pond and in every lotus flower three wonderfully beautiful women were sitting. Thus Phra In came down to earth into the land of Chomputhovip, which is Siam. There was a lovely forest there in which were living four hermits. The god came down from his elephant, greeted the hermits and told them that the highest god had given him the order to build a splendid royal city for the future master on Earth. The hermits, however, were already been living one hundred thousand years in this place and told the god Phra In that the area was very suitable for the foundation of a city. There was also a forest in the vicinity in which there was a temple to the gods. Phra In was very happy with this good news and gave his architect Vishnukam the assignment to build the city immediately. Upon the latter's order a great earthquake shook the area and three enclosure walls grew out of the ground with a splendid royal palace and all the buildings which come with a royal city. Phra In flew again to the throne of Sayompuvanat and reported that the city built according to his order was ready. The highest god gave the future king the name Anomatan. As weapon he gave him a bow of magical powers as a gift and a throwing-wheel and a trident.[11] He also equipped him with all the power and wisdom which a king needs. In addition Anomatan received a first queen and 65,000 secondary wives who rivaled with each other in beauty. Upon this Sayompuvanat with his entire retinue let himself be carried on the bird Krut to the newly built royal city. The city received the name Ayuthia. A lot of people crowded in the streets of the city and trade and commerce was flourishing.

Even if this legend is not believed word for word by the Siamese it still explains best the position that is taken by the king in Siam. The Siamese indeed consider themselves the most important people of the Earth and their kings today still claims a godly veneration, which the people accord them willingly. They have their name from King Rama, a reincarnation of Vishnu. The present king has the name Rama VI and has expressly conferred the name Rama upon his direct predecessor. This is however nothing new but the consequence of the Siamese worldview.

On the gable of the Siamese temple they often depict Phra Narai riding on the bird Krut. Phra Narai is the Siamese form of Narayana, a designation of the god Vishnu. With this representation are symbolically meant the kings of Siam. Even today on the postage stamps the head of the king carried by a Garuda is shown. Because the latter, the king of the birds, is the mount of the god Vishnu, the relationships are also clear here. In all reports on Siam it is pointed out with what a godly veneration the Siamese encounter their king. Only since the conclusion of the newest trade treaties is the old Siamese ceremonial gradually becoming more flexible.

Formerly, every Siamese in the presence of the king had to throw themselves on the floor, with their face to the floor and hands folded above their heads. The reports of earlier envoys are full of descriptions of these customs, which are so alien to Europeans. Crawfurd writes about an audience with the king: "Every corner of this great hall was so filled with court servants lying down on their knees that it was difficult to get only a step ahead without stepping on any of them." De la Loubère reports: "The few prominent mandarins are sitting uncovered in the courtyards or gardens and if they notice from certain signs that the king sees them they all throw themselves down on knees and elbows even when they do not see him themselves." In relation to a festive parade de la Loubère says: "If the king stops, all who follow him throw themselves down on their knees and arms and those who are riding on horses or

elephants fall forwards flat out on these animals."

Nobody can be situated physically higher than the king. Formerly, when he sailed on one of his great rowing boats on a canal underneath a bridge, traffic on the busy streets stopped immediately because nobody dared to go across the bridge as long as a royal rowing boat was under it. When the king moved around outside the palace in the streets, quite a number of windows had to be closed. In the front part of the rowing boat of the king even today there stands an employee with bow and arrow. Formerly, it was his duty to shoot down everybody who did not throw himself down for the king.

Because the king also was the highest feudal lord and all the land his property, based on his perfect and all embracing power he can distribute wealth and property and elevate simple people to higher ranks and also lower their status again. The people are so caught in the traditions that they do not think about the introduction of a parliament or about abolishing this patriarchal situation.

Because since times past the proceeds of the whole kingdom are at the disposal of the king, the royal household was always very ostentatious. The kings of Siam hold a community of Brahmins in high honors since time immemorial. They are of direct Indian descent and do not mix with other people. They are assigned to ensure that celebrations at the royal court are held at the right time and in the right manner. The kings have the holy duty to bring the country blessings and wealth by correctly upholding these celebrations.[12]

The Rek Na Feast

Formerly the king held the plowing and the harvest feasts. Today other officials are assigned this. De la Loubère already reported that for this a special official was used. The

Brahmin astrologers fix the exact date only just before the beginning of the festivities, which always fall in the first half of May. Today the Minister of Agriculture has the duty in the place of the king to lead the plow and sow the first rice of the year. Formerly, he had a right to the entire proceeds of the whole kingdom for one day during which he was considered a king. He is accompanied on the field by a great procession. He goes, followed by the Brahmin priests, into a hall especially built for the feast. The Brahmins consecrate a couple of oxen adorned with flowers by sprinkling water on them and other symbolic rites. They are yoked to the richly decorated plow. The minister leads them for about an hour around the field. Four older ladies of the royal family, carrying baskets with consecrated rice follow him. They sow the rice on the plowed land. The oxen must pull the plow back and forth nine times between two fixed posts. Then they are unyoked. Several fruits are offered them and the belief exists that there will be a shortage in the coming year of the fruit which they eat most. Furthermore, the people also watch the *pha nung* of the minister when he plows. If it is hanging a little too low then there will be little rain in the coming year, if it is pulled up too high the country is threatened with an inundation. If, however, the cloth is hanging at the correct height between the ankle and the knee then the flood will be normal and there will be a good harvest. After the completion of the plowing the farmers jump on the field to obtain a few grains of rice which they then mix with their own seed. This is considered to bring extraordinary luck.

Song Khran

The Brahmin astrologers at the court of the king calculate in advance the day on which the sun comes out of the zodiac sign of pisces and enters that of Aries in order to celebrate the Song Khran feast, which is the New Year celebration of the old Siamese sun year, while the Krut Thai days of festivities fall somewhat together with the European New Year in January.

During this celebration the Buddha statues are submerged into consecrated water and sprinkled with it. The women draw the water, bathe the Buddha statue of their house altar, and their grandparents and elderly relatives in order to obtain merit. Today the ceremonial bath of priests and elderly people is symbolized by offerings of bottles of fragrant water, handkerchiefs and other gifts.

The king invites on this day the high officials and the leadership of the monkshood to his palace for a great feast. In the palace, he takes a ritual bath, the hour of which is very care-fully calculated by the Brahmin astrologers.

The laymen receive the priests, go for special religious festivities to the temple, visit each other and do honor to games of chance. In the villages the custom has been preserved that during the Song Khran feast people sprinkle each other with water.

The Water of Allegiance

Twice a year the officials of the king must swear loyalty by drinking the water of allegiance, specifically at the beginning of the summer and winter half-year. Presently, by order of the present king, the feast is held only once, shortly after the beginning of the spring. The practice goes back to a passage of the Ramakien in which Pipek, a brother of King Totsakan, defects to Phra Ram. Because they do not trust him he must drink the water of allegiance. The invincible weapons of Phra Ram are submerged into the water and Pipek must swear an oath that these weapons would destroy him if he would break his oath. In the same way even today the Brahmin priests submerge swords, daggers, lances as well as a bronze statue of Vishnu in the water that has been displayed in great bronze basins in the temple of the royal palace. All princes, nobles and higher-ranking officials must drink the water in front of the king. The lower-ranking officials perform this ceremony in their respective administrative offices before their minister. This water is also sent in sealed barrels to the provinces. There the ceremony is held in front of the governor. The Buddhist priests do not drink the water of allegiance. By virtue of the sanctity of their function they are freed from this ceremony. The chief monks of the capital and its close vicinity, however, hold in connection with this ceremony a special feast in the Vat Phra Keo temple. At this celebration the king sits before the main Buddha statue with his face turned towards the East. The officers and military officials present themselves on the right side, the civil officials on the left side. If they do not wear their military uniform they are dressed in bright white clothes, also the *pha nung*, shoes and socks are white, at the most interwoven with gold. Coat and belt are especially beautiful and richly adorned with gold embroidery. The officials step alone in front of the king who sits on his throne, take a small chalice with the consecrated water, wet their fronts and drink the rest. Some also shake the last drops over their heads. (Formerly, immediately after this feast the official salaries were paid out.)

This feast coincided earlier with the Buddhist festive days of Khao Wasa and Ok Wasa.

Lo Ching Cha

While the Rek Na feast is a spring feast and indicates the beginning of tillage, in autumn some kind of harvest feast is held which is called the feast of the swing. With a great festive parade and with great pomp the minister for agriculture is brought to the square in Bangkok on which the Giant Swing is erected. There he takes his place in a pavilion that has been covered with white muslin, which has been set up for this purpose only. Formerly, he had to stand on his feet during the whole feast and the others could not sit on the ground. Presently he takes his place in an armchair and places one leg over his knee and he has the other foot on the ground. Four Brahmin priests, two each on the right and the left side, accompany him. If he touched the ground with the lifted foot before three games had ended, the Brahmins were formerly allowed to rob him of his property. The priests and the swingers are dressed in white during the feast. The latter also have on their heads a tight, cone-shaped white cap with a very long tip. The swing is only hung up during the three festive days and every year shorter by two inches. If one day the swing is too short to swing, then the end of this period of world history has come close according to Brahmin beliefs. In front of the swing a bamboo post has been fixed to which a bag with *ticals* has been tied. The swingers must grab this with their teeth. When this has been accomplished three times, the Brahmin priests draw consecrated water into a bull's horn and sprinkle it over the people. According to their beliefs, this blesses the people. In the festive parade many symbols and objects are carried along which refer to the relationship of the feast with the harvest and which depict some kind of expression of gratitude for the rice sheaves which have been collected during the harvest.

Totkatin

In the month of October the King, the Court and the whole population visit the temples. At this occasion the monks are presented new yellow habits, their dress for the coming year. The festivities last an entire month. The king visits a series of royal temples, partly along the water, partly on land, but the water processions are conducted with very special displays of splendor. Because the king cannot reach all the temples which have been founded by him or his predecessors, he sends officials to the more distant ones who present gifts in his name to the temple. Today, these splendid processions take place with a great presence of military men.

When the great Totkatin procession reaches a temple, first a few yellow cloths are brought before the door and an official informs the monks that the king wishes to visit the temple and present gifts. The king's cortege takes it's place on both sides of the entrance and the king is accompanied to the door by Siamese music, blowing conches and horns. The military musical bands play the national anthem. When the king has reached the temple door he takes a stack of priest's habits, carries them on both his hands into the temple and places them on a table that is ready. On the latter five gold flower vases, five gold platters with roasted rice, five gold candelabras and five incense sticks are standing. The king kneels before the altar and reveres the Buddhist trinity: the Lord Buddha, the Buddha's teachings and Buddha's community. He prays for happiness and blessing for the whole kingdom in the coming year. When he stands up again he addresses the chief monk with the request to accept his renewed vow to fulfill the five rules of the Buddhist religion. These are: (1) to kill no living being; (2) not to oppress any human being; (3) not to take a women, who belongs to someone else, as his own as long as there is even the smallest resistance from the woman, her parents or relatives; (4) not to lie and not to falsely fight people or to use insulting language; (5) not to take intoxicating liquids. After the renewal of this vow the king presents his gifts to the temple's priests upon which the latter reply in Pali *"sadhu, sadhu."* The chief priest then speaks to the community of monks: "These *pha katin* (monks' habits) have been given by the king who has descended and come here himself in his extraordinary goodness and rectitude to give these clothes to us, a community of Buddhist priests—without designating any special person who should wear them." Upon this, the priests distribute the habits and other gifts among themselves, bow humbly and venerate the Buddha while they recite a Pali chant. Besides the clothes the priests received other gifts which they need for their livelihood such as blankets, table utensils and boats. After he has once more venerated the Buddhist trinity, the king then leaves the temple while the priests pronounce a Pali blessing over him.

For the procession on the water the great royal rowing boats are used which are built in the shape of dragons. In front is a dragon or snake head which stands up high above the water. The end of the boat is lengthened into a great, lifted dragon tail (se Plate 117). The boats are moved by 80 to 100 oarsmen who have practiced for months to work in unison very precisely. The boatsmen wear red uniforms embroidered with gold and they use gilded oars. In the middle of the boat stands a great baldachin under which the king, dressed in old-Siamese clothes, takes his place. In front of the king the boats of the high notables sail; the king is followed by the boats of the princes of the royal houses and of the queens and by the boat with the gifts for the monasteries. These processions have been held for hundreds of years in the same way. Jodocus Schouten (1636) describes one of them as follows: "Since many years past it is the custom that in the month of October of every year the king of Siam, dressed as a triumpher, shows himself to the people with great splendor and pomp on the water and on land at which the princes, notables and nobility of the whole country, all similarly dressed in the most expensive costumes, accompany him.

"On this day, the king also visits the temple of the gods in which he exhausts himself in prayers for his and his peoples' great welfare and wealth and to which he brings many gifts. This festive procession is usually ordered as follows: first march from the royal palace to the main temple a row of about 200 elephants on each of which three armed men are sitting. Then come many musicians with gongs, flutes and hand timpani and at the same time 1,000 heavily armed soldiers with shields. Behind these follow in the right rank order all the great men of the kingdom on horses, some glittering with gold diadems and all of them with a retine of 60, 80 or 100 men on foot. Behind this comes the bodyguard of the king, about 200 Japanese with beautiful weapons and flags and a musical band with varied instruments. Horses and elephants are glittering with precious stones. They are followed under the sounds of a lovely music by many servants of the royal court overloaded with fruits and gifts, which have to be brought to the temples. Then come a lot of the country's nobles with folded hands and a few princes adorned with diadems one of whom is bearing the gold royal standard and another the gold sword of justice. And then appears in his full splendor, dressed in precious clothes, His Royal Majesty himself, seated on a beautiful elephant under a gold baldachin which is carried by on the shoulders of porters, and surrounded with throngs of high-ranking men and courtiers. The king is followed by the Prince or Crown Prince with his courtiers. Behind him come the women and secondary women of the king with the whole harem, all of them seated under small baldachins, which are carried by elephants. Many court officials and 600 armed soldiers concluded the parade. In all, some 15,000 to 16,000 people participate in such a festive parade.

"On the water however the rank ordering is the following. The parade is opened by about 200 men of high nobility, each in their own boat seated under a gilded tent-shaped superstructure, with 60 to 80 oarsmen. They are followed by four ships with musicians of all varieties and then, in order to increase the splendor, 50 ships of the king with painted gilded cabins and with 80 to 90 oarsmen. Then follow, each with 90 to 100 oarsmen, ten artful precious boats that are completely gilded like their oars. In the most beautiful one the king is seated like the statue of a god under a gilded baldachin and at his feet many notables with an expression of the deepest veneration in their posture and on their faces. In the back of the boat a specific official of the king, who holds the gilded royal shield, has his place. Then follows the princely brother of the king, the Crown Prince with his Court retinue, all seated under gilded baldachins and in silk tents. The women of the king join them; every one sails in her own boat, and then the harem. At the end still come many boats with court officials and nobles so that the whole parade consists of about 400 to 500 boats and counts not less than about 25,000 to 30,000 people.

"The banks of the river on both sides are covered with many carriages and an uncountable crowd who show the king their veneration and respect in the most submissive manner and with bowed heads and folded hands."

Loi Kathong

In accordance with an ancient Indian custom the lantern feast is also held in Siam; it takes place about the month of October. It is of Brahmin origins and is celebrated to soothe the spirits of the water. A lot of fireworks are lit and small boats made of banana leaves with burning wax candles are placed on the Menam River as gifts. In Bangkok, especially in the vicinity of the palace, the many lights flaming up everywhere and mirrored in the water make the night into a day. The river is animated by sailing ships, rafts, boats and floating logs on which burning lights are placed. They float about on the waves loaded with gifts to the god of the water, which consist of betel, tobacco, rice, sugar and sweets. They thank the god for the merciful protection during the past year and offer these gifts for gratitude and as expiatory sacrifices because one has been bathing unharmed in its waters, because one has drunk its sweet water the whole year long and because the boats have rowed without danger over the depths of the rivers. Decorated royal boats sail on the river during this time. Lotus flowers with burning wax candles are an especially beloved gift and also small floats made of the trunk of banana trees that are adorned with flowers, flags and wax candles. Thousands of people are on the river during the night. This feast is celebrated the same way in every province. The inhabitants of the coast place their gifts on the waves at the sea banks. The king and the courtiers themselves place such boats on the water.

In the course of time the original Brahmin celebration has been subsumed under the Buddhist festive day. During the three nights Buddhist preaching and readings from the sacred books are held. Even among the Siamese the recollection has been preserved that this celebration refers indeed to the Ganges River, the holy Ganga. In their opinion the boats with the lights are placed on the river to beg for remission from Nang Thorani (this is the Goddess of the Earth) and Nang Kongkhla (this is the Goddess of the Water). Kongkhla apparently is identical to Ganga.

However, pious Siamese give as reason for these feasts that on a distant shore there is a footprint of the Buddha to whom these offerings of fire are brought.

Birth, Enlightenment and Death of Buddha

According to Siamese traditions the three greatest events in the life of Buddha on earth—birth, attainment of the state of Buddha and birth, attainment of the state of Buddha and death after 80 years of age—fall on the same day of the year. Therefore they are celebrated together. The religious aspect of the feast takes precedence because one visits the temple and one accomplishes meritorious works. They present gifts to the poor, bring offers to Buddha images and monks, say prayers and hear songs of praise. In the evening of the second day the temples are lit up with candles, lanterns and torches.

Other Buddhist festive days are the Khao Wasa and Ok Wasa celebrations. Wasa is a Pali word and it means rain. Buddha already gave the monks the advice not to walk around during this time. It is the period of the Buddhist fasting time or self-denial. For the monks in the monasteries these are the months of repentance and self-abasement. The beginning and the end of the rainy season are celebrated. At the end of the rainy season the priests are regaled. From the gifts during this celebration Siamese lay people expect a special merit for their future reincarnations. They believe that every gift and every bit of food which they present to the priests during these feasts will be rewarded them a hundredfold in the next reincarnation.

Krut Thai (Siamese New Year)

At the Siamese New Year feast cannons are brought all around the royal palace at night. They are loaded with strips of palm leaf on which soothing maxims and magical formulae, powerful against demons, have been scratched. In the second night the cannons are fired after each other in all directions of Heaven. From each cannon 36 shots are fired. This happens in order to chase the evil spirits to the boundaries of the city. Because the people outside the city also wish to participate in these celebrations, they take part in the firing so that one can hear artillery pieces from the vicinity being fired all night long. The Buddhist priests are placed on the city wall in order to banish the evil spirits with their collective prayers. Afterwards they pull a white, seven-fold cotton thread around the merlons of the whole city wall and around the walls of the palace which constitutes a city by itself.

Court and population celebrate this feast with great merry-making, visit the temples and bring flower, incense and candle offerings to Buddha images. The religious festivities take the first two days; on the third day the whole population indulges in games of chance which are prohibited during the rest of the year.

Music

Siamese music is very different from ours. While our diatonic scale is based on the so-called natural or basic tones, which stand in clear numeric ratios to each other such as 1:2, 1:3, 1:4, 1:5, 1:6, 1:8, 1:9, 1:10, 1:12, 1:15, etc., Siamese music recognizes of these intervals only the ratio of the frequency 1:2 from the basic tone to the octavo. In European music this octavo is sub-divided in twelve equal intervals or halftones while here it is sub-divided in seven full, equal tones. This would thus be equivalent to 14 halftones. Halftones are however unknown in Siam. Therefore, there is no key signature and no different keys.

The main instrument in the orchestra is the *ganat*, a xylophone, which comprises three octavos and the claviature of which has been hung from two strings over a boat-shaped box. The individual wooden little bars are tuned by gluing on pieces of wax. A first and second *ganat* is distinguished. Besides this, first and second violins, *siso ek* and *sit to,* are used. An instrument that corresponds with our cello is the *takeh,* which lies flat on the ground. The violins are placed on the ground like our cellos. In addition there are flutes, shawms, trumpets without keys, a great number of percussion instruments, timpani, drums, also batteries of timpani and gongs at which the musician sits in the middle of the instruments which have been set up in a half-circle around him.

The musicians all sit on the ground with their legs tucked under, their instruments in front of them. A Siamese writing of notes does not exist. The musicians must know the partly very long musical pieces by heart. Thus all Siamese orchestras, however numerous, are without musical conductors.

While in European music the melody is accompanied by certain chords according to the laws of harmony, in Siam all the instruments usually play in unison with the exception of the percussion instruments, especially the gongs and the great timpani. Fourth movements are also known. Then they play a theme that is repeated in numerous variations. Because Siamese music cannot find pleasure in harmonies, their only way of expression lies in the melody which has many more ornaments and embellishments than ours. There are many types of trills, appoggiatura and fixed figures. One could compare the completion of the lines of the melodies with the mostly gracious curves of Siamese decorative figures. Just as we cannot clearly and sharply recognize Siamese decorations in their subtlety at first sight, so it mostly happens for us Europeans too with the very lively lines of Siamese melodies. In addition, most musical pieces are played in, for us, a relatively very fast movement. Only towards the end of the piece the melody is slower and more elevated. With the *ganat* continuing tones are indicated with tremolo just as with our xylophone. Usually the sequence of the tones is so fast that a simple strike of the bar is sufficient. The changes in tempo are sometimes stunning and surprising. Long-winded melodies find less approval with the Siamese listener and they are therefore very rare.

Knowledge of music belongs to the requirements that are set for every Siamese educated person. Formerly, the young folk of both sexes in the better families were required to know by heart a fixed number of musical pieces. The number of such pieces grew with the rank of the person.

Theater performances are always staged with musical accompaniments; the same is true for dances and ballet, which are part of the theater plays.

The Lao of Upper Siam as well as several other peoples of the hill tribes play the Lao flute or organ. This is an instrument consisting of reed flutes (see Plate 54).

In the various parades of the Totkatin processions one can see Siamese musicians whose instruments are carried on bamboo poles. At cremation festivities a special mourning music is played during the procession. It consists mostly of a flute which plays a mourning melody in long sustained tones while in certain intervals it is accompanied by timpani and hand drums (see Plate 76).

The Siamese are very musical and have a great love for music. It is widespread in all classes of society. The king, the princes and the notables maintain special house orchestras.

Theater

The achievements of the Siamese in respect to theater are quite considerable. The whole population have a very great aptitude for mime art and dance. Even children often imitate dances as they are staged in theater. They show great grace and an inborn sense for beauty and elegant movement, which has a peculiar style as is also expressed in Siamese decoration.

There are several kinds of theater plays, first of all the Khon or Lakon plays, Likae theater, shadow-play (*nang*) and marionette-play (*hun*).[13]

The Khon plays only treat the mimic staging of the heroic Ramakien epic, the Siamese version of the Indian Ramayana. The stage is square. The spectators sit on three sides; on the fourth a wall with three towers rises up. There are no wings in the old theater. The theater players come on stage in splendid costumes; the players of male roles mostly wear masks covering their heads. It goes together with the personages of the Ramakien story. […] Here we only mention that in the Ramakien the struggles of King Phra Ram, who has allied himself with the king of the monkeys against Totsakan, the prince of demons and giants, are depicted. The city of the king of the giants is besieged and conquered after a long struggle of Phra Ram and his allies. The struggle of light against darkness is represented symbolically in which the good powers, personified in Phra Ram, gain the upper hand.

The staging book distinguishes three kinds of personages, which are depicted very clearly in the three books: Manusaphong (the human race), Vanaraphong (the monkey race) and Asuraphong (the race of the giants). Because several heroes have green, red, gold and other facial colors, complete head-masks are required. Only the main players of the female parts such as the wife of Phra Ram and a few others, do not wear any facial masks but make themselves up. From this is clear that the players of demons and of monkey warriors must wear masks, which go along with their roles. As make-up they use white color powder which has been mixed with fine coconut oil and sticks very tightly to the skin. Taking off the make-up takes a disproportionately long time.

The costumes usually show very expensive embroideries and are covered with rich decorations and real gold specks. In addition, the players wear a lot of jewelry. Until very recently it was the custom that the king, the princes, the nobles and the notables kept their own theater in which their wives played. They are clearly distinguishable from the players prancing about. The artistic achievements in the private theaters are higher than those in the public theater; indeed, one can even conclude that art and culture are the more developed the closer they come to the royal court.

The common theaters are led by a director, whose wives play the leading parts. While in private theaters only women play, in the common theater men and women play together. The theater troops are hired for a fixed amount and a series of performances. The prominent and rich Siamese have theater troops play for the people during their feasts.

Most grandiose were such plays at royal cremations on the open courtyard in front of the palace. Such performances at funeral celebrations are today no longer common.

The Siamese find it beautiful when women have slender limbs and their joints can bend backwards very far, especially the fingers bending backwards and if possible the whole hand moving very far backwards to the lower arm. In order to reinforce this impression of bending backwards further, the theater players sometimes have lengthened, silver or gold fingernails which are bent backwards. Formerly their use was general.

The expensive jewelry of the theater players in the private theaters exceeds any Europeans imagination. Every theater player is adorned with a great fortune in jewelry. The costumes are not buttoned up but sewn on very tightly. They show off the beautiful bodylines and the gracious movements of the supple female players especially graphically. In the private theaters it is common that the master of the house has placed next to him a platter of jewelry or money. He lets a servant hand a theater player a gift for an especially good performance. The play is then interrupted for a moment and the recipient of the gift bows with hands folded in front towards the presenter.

In plays of large troops the players stay mute and represent the actions with mime and dances. Every side has a speaker, who recites words and replies for every theater player. On the right side of the spectators the orchestra is seated, on the left the choir of old women. They hold long wooden poles in their hands and bang them to indicate the measure to the choir songs, who recite in a semi-singing voice.

While in the Khon plays only episodes of the Ramakien can be played, in Lakon also other themes, borrowed from the world of saga and fairy tales, can be treated. The theater players speak in this kind of play but only the choir songs are fixed. Only the general train of action is prescribed to the theater players and the development of the scenes is left to their talents of improvisation. Thus a Siamese can see a play again and again because, according to the experience of the player, it will always be new and different.

Siamese dramas are very long and mostly they cannot be played to the end in a single evening. The duration of a play usually stretches three or five evenings and only during moonlit nights, while during the dark half of the month the theater troop rests.

In Likae plays only men perform. They play comedies, mostly with rude and erotic jokes, which stir the laughing muscles of the spectators a lot. In general, Likae is improper and prominent Siamese do not watch these kind of plays.

The Siamese are eager theatergoers and do not shy away from the proportionally high entrance fees. Especially brilliant are the accompanying ballets and mimic dances. The female players dance calmly without hurried movements. Only free dancing is allowed and only by women. The movements are mostly executed with the torso and arms. The weapons and accessories used in these dances are adorned with mosaics of mirror glass and reflect the light of the lamps in a multitude of refractions. To this must be added the splendid effects of the rich wrought ironwork which is studded with precious stones. In common theaters they are replaced by inlaid mirror mosaics.

Carl Stumpf, who saw a Siamese theater troop in Berlin, wrote about it: "In the public performances the women sang and danced while the men built the orchestra. The costumes of the dancers were extraordinarily splendid, admirable in shades and harmony of colors, the movements at first strange for us but very refined, i.e., the multitude, boldness and expressiveness of the hand movements astonished us. In comparison with such a virtuoso mimic of the hands we can find weak approaches only on our stages, but we could gain the conviction here that they deserve at least as much as the legs to be cultured."

In the shadow-plays there are figures of various sizes. Among the largest ones, the Nang Luang, the figures are somewhat larger than life-size and cut from buffalo skin. They are moveable and tied in such a way to bamboo sticks that they can be led across the screen by a single bearer. In the background an 18 meter long, two to three meters high linen wall has been erected, behind which a huge, open fire is maintained. The spectators sit at the side away from the fire. All figures that are needed for a play are laid flat on the ground in order of use. The bearers of the shadow-play figures wait in the dark for a given sign and then they suddenly appear before the linen. When doing this their shadow works with them and their gracious movement are an integral part of the shadow-play.

Mostly episodes of the Ramakien are shown. On one side they imagine Langka, the capital of the king of the giants, and on the other side the tent camp of king Rama. The verses of the epic are recited in a festive singing tone by a speaker and the shadow-play figures are moved according to the train of action. There are about two thousand figures and scenes played from the Ramakien, all cut from leather

according to an old fixed tradition. The figures of the Nang Luang are mostly two meters high. They are masterful in their movements, and in fine finishing of detail they are masterpieces of decorative art.

Shadow-play performances are usually played during cremation ceremonies. Since today the pleasurable parts are limited at cremations the shadow-play theater is very much in decline and it is threatened with complete disappearance. Formerly the king, the princes and prominent people all had a set of large figures in their possession. The directors of the professional theater players had smaller sets, which they also showed for paid orders.

Derived from the shadow-plays are the Nang Thalung, which can move head, limbs and lips like the Javanese Vajang figures. The theater players who stage the figures, speak and give replies. They are mostly to be found on the Malay Peninsula in the vicinity of Nakon Sri Thammarat.

To conclude, we still have to deal with the marionette-plays, which are completely similar in technique to ours. Mostly the Rama plays are staged here. The marionettes, especially those of the royal plays, are true masterpieces of Siamese handicraft because in masks and jewelry they display a minia-turized refinery of ornaments.

Next to these purely Siamese theaters the Annamese lantern-dances, Chinese Ngiu and also Burmese and Malay shadow-plays are beloved.

Notes to the Plates

What an excellent role the canals and the waterways of south Siam play and how busy the traffic on them is, is depicted by **Plates 1-11**. **Plates 1-3** show canal landscapes in the neighborhood of the capital. On **Plate 1** we see several staircases coming from the canal to the houses which are fully hidden in the vegetation. On the left side of the plate stand the slender areca palms, straight as arrows and which furnish betel nuts, on the right the more bent coconut palms.

Plate 4. A view of Bangkok. The photo is made from the gallery of the great Phra Prang tower of the Vat Arun temple. It provides a beautiful view over the Menam River to the royal palace with its numerous, tower-like slender roofs.

The English diplomat Crawfurd, who visited Siam in the spring of 1822, describes arriving in Bangkok as follows: "Bangkok, the capital, which is located on both banks of the Menam, provides an interesting impression from the distance. Many temples of the Lord Buddha with their high towers, most of them glittering with gilding, stick out above the low huts and shanty dwellings of the inhabitants. Palm trees and common fruit trees are planted in-between in great quantities. On both sides of the river there is a row of floating houses, which rest on bamboo rafts tied up to the bank. These appear to be the cleanest and best houses in which prominent Chinese merchants are living. Next to these water houses the greatest local ships were moored.

The throng of crisscrossing boats and launches, of all kinds and sizes, gave the river a very animated appearance. The number of these surprised us in the beginning greatly because we did not know yet that Bangkok has little or no streets but that the river and the canals constitute the usual streets, not only for cargo transport but also for any kind of people. Many of these boats are used as shops for utensils, smoked fish, fresh pork and such things. Salesmen of these establishments shout their wares like in a European town." (See also **Plate 5-10**).

Plate 5. A canal near the Vat Rajabophit temple in Bangkok. The canal passes in front of the part of the temple in which the funeral *phra chedi* of the royal princes are located. While some of these follow the ancient architectural shapes of Angkor Vat, some others have been erected in gothic style during the era of King Chulalongkorn, others still as renaissance buildings; luckily the copying of foreign styles in Siamese temple architecture has been tempered.

Plate 8. A canal scene in Bangkok at the time of ebb-tide. During this time the water stands so low that the houses are separated from the fairway by great mud banks which one cannot cross by foot. Such houses are sometimes only accessible during flood tide.

Plate 9 shows how intense the traffic in the individual canals is; here shown in a scene at market time in the Bangkok Noi canal. Despite the great thronging of people there are never quarrels or fighting and life on the canals goes on very quietly even during the most hectic times.

Plate 11. Pilgrims in boats near the Phra Chedi Klang Nam. Every year great feasts take place near this famous temple. From far and wide uncountable pilgrims in boats arrive and they venerate the temple, which lies on an artificial isle, by sailing three times around it. At this time there are also boat races.

The predilection of the Siamese for living near water is general. Such a location has great advantages for them because then they are at the same time on the great water streets of the country and from there can visit their neighbors easily and conveniently. The river also removes all the dirt. In addition, the Siamese like to bathe very often and do so. **Plate 12** shows a typical Siamese dwelling on a canal in the Menam plain. **Plate 13** shows a Siamese pile dwelling on a canal in Bangkok Noi. These pile dwellings take the various heights of the water into account. Also this way of building is in the tropical climate of Siam very healthy because the breeze can blow underneath the house. The better houses are built from teakwood. The cleanly finished walls of wooden half-timber show interesting samples of columns and crossbeams. The roofs are covered with the leaves of the attap palm, which divert heat and rain to the same degree. The house usually has a low veranda in front. The pile dwelling of the Siamese appears to have evolved especially on the banks in a muddy vicinity. This form of building is also used by them, as in **Plate 14**, when the house is built completely on dry land. On the gable one can notice the characteristic snake-heads which are stylized so strongly on ordinary dwellings that they are barely recognizable as such and only consist of an arched, cut-out light piece of wood.

Plate 15 shows a Siamese house with a double gable on a square floater. Such floating houses are in Siam very much loved, as are boathouses (**Plate 16** and **17**). In the last plate one can see a canal in Ayuthia on which only a small fairway has been left free by the houseboats and the floating houses.

Plate 18 shows the market traffic in front of the bazaar of floating houses on the Menam bank. Bastian (*Reisen in Siam*, page 61) reported about this: "The most important traffic of Bangkok does not take place on land but on the water, because on both sides of the river a double row of floating houses frames the bank and builds the great market in which the most industrious part of the population gathers daily. Every house is open on the side directed to the river and constitutes by the things placed there an open shop which one can inspect conveniently to select what is needed when floating by. Usually the craftsmen live together in the same area in order that one can obtain an overview of the stocks. In-between are sales boats which have brought fresh fruits, fish, vegetables, etc."

Lower Siam with the Menam plain is completely flat without any soil elevations. **Plate 20** shows a group of houses in the village of Khlong Rangsit, located on a canal, on which a travel boat sails away with strong South-South-West monsoon.

Plate 21 also provides a view of the flat plain of Menam. On both sides of the canals unending flat rice fields stretch out. On the other hand the upper river course is hemmed in by high mountains (see **Plate 18** below and **Plate 19**).

The whole of the Lao States is a great mountainous country. **Plate 22** provides an example of the landscape in the vicinity of Khao Phyng, while **Plate 23** shows a mountain range from the southern peninsula. Near the temple on the mountain peak the *phra chedi* lies on the summit of the whole mountain, while the main building lies somewhat lower and even further down from the other monastery buildings.

Plate 26. A Siamese woman of King Mongkut's era. According to old traditions the clothes are the same for women and men in Siam. Both wear a *pha nung*, which are wide, wrinkled shorts of one great piece of cloth. Formerly, men and women went about with naked torsos. Among the prominent Siamese women, however, it was the custom to cover up the breast with a piece of cloth that left the right shoulder and the right arm free. The *pha nung* was kept in place by a belt. Characteristic is the old hairdo of the Siamese. Formerly they shaved their heads and only left a round spot on top of the head where they wore the hair sticking up like a brush. The women cut their hair short, instead of shaving them off and they wore the same circular hair tuft as the men.

The oarsman in **Plate 27** also had this hairdo. Striking is the pointed rhomboid-shaped oar. In the background of the picture one can see a few sugar cane clumps.

Under the government of King Chulalongkorn the Siamese males and females wore their hair combed backwards without shaving any parts of their heads (**Plate 29-31**). While formerly only prominent women wore a breast shawl, after King Chulalongkorn returned from Europe, he issued a regulation that all women had to wear a shawl.

The women of the Peguans or Mons have always worn their hair long (**Plate 32**), as was the case for the Thai Yai or Lao (**Plate 33-41**). The hair is tied together in the most varied buns and hairdos. As clothes, except for a small jacket, they have a skirt with transverse or longitudinal stripes. In **Plate 33** the grandmother carries her grandchild on the hip. In Siam this is called "to support the strength."

Plate 56. A Shan ox caravan crossing over the Khao Phyng. The Shan come every year to the markets of Phrabat. The pilgrims from the south of Siam are attracted there by the great religious feasts while the Shan bring bronze gongs, drums, knives, weapons and cloth from the North to sell there.

Plate 62, top: a festive parade of Lao, Petchaburi. While the Lao only live in the North, a colony of them settled in the vicinity of Petchaburi on the Malay Peninsula as the consequence of a war. They have their own customs and traditions strictly maintained for centuries.

Plate 62 bottom to **Plate 71**. The elephant howdahs have a large, strongly jutting sunroof that is especially clear in **Plate 64**. The saddles shown in **Plate 65** have unusual shapes. They are used at the royal festivities. In order to give the princes who ride on the elephants a free view they have four great arched openings.

In Siam elephants do not breed in captivity but they have to be caught. In the vicinity of Ayuthia they still have the old elephant kraal to organize the elephant hunts which has remained in use even after the sacking of the city.

The strength the working elephants possess is shown in **Plate 67**. In **Plate 70** war elephants have had two lines painted straight like a candle on their fronts. The tusks of war elephants are often inserted into metal rings in order to protect them from splintering. (**Plate 71**).

Plate 72. The edifices for the cremation festivities of King Mongkut (deceased 1868) on the Phramen grounds (royal cremation site) north of the great city palace of Bangkok. The photo shows the main group of the Phramen with the proper Mount Meru in the middle. The Siamese call the edifice in which the cremation of the royal body takes place Mount Meru in imitation of the ancient Indian world system. With this they assume that the body of the king burns to ashes on the highest summit in the middle point of the world. The height of the edifice up to the highest top was about 60 meters. On all four sides the roofs are stacked on top of each other; all of them ending in strongly bent snake-heads; the whole structure is overloaded with an unbelievable splendor of gold ornaments, mosaics of mirror glass and the richest ornaments. The main edifice is surrounded by eight buildings on the eight points of the compass. All these buildings are crowned with delightful *phra prang* spires. Uncountable umbrellas with nine and eleven layers glittering with gold and silver surround the proud building. Demonic giant figures protect the entrances as tower guards.

Plate 73. Edifices for the cremation of two princes in the reign of King Chulalongkorn. This photo was taken from the tower of the Ministry of Justice, since then torn down, at the time the funeral procession with the urn containing the ashes arrived in front of the eastern portico and the great throng following the funeral was circling thrice around the main building. Because this photo was taken from a height, one can see behind the buildings for the cremation the edifices of the Vat Mahathat temple, behind it the Menam River and the opposite bank. In Vat Mahathat one can clearly distinguish between the great religious edifices and the small houses of the monks quarters situated on the left side.

Outside the great building for the royal cremation there are still many theaters, restaurants and other buildings erected. Two of the same can be seen right and left of the portico building.

Plate 74. Buildings for the cremation of a prince in the reign of King Chulalongkorn. The photo shows the middle part of the main building of a Phramen edifice. Exceptionally the main building has two stories. The main room in the middle, in which the cremation takes place, is characterized by the highest *mondob* (a tower-like edifice with a strongly elongated spire) with seven stories. On all sides, astride the roofs, similar towers with five stories surround it. On the four corners of the main building smaller buildings with a similar crown are springing up. All details are decorated with delightful gilded ornaments. These edifices, which are destined for the cremation of the royal family, are of the most splendid ever invented by human imagination. They are usually more beautiful and daring in their conception than the temple architecture built to last. Built to be used only for a very short time they disappear like dream images.

Plate 75. At the cremation ceremony of King Chulalongkorn, March 1911. The middle part of the Phramen edifices. In the middle of the whole complex, supported by four great wooden posts, rises the stately, high baldachin completely covered with gold. Under it lies the real cremation place to which wide staircases lead up. The king, the queen, the princes and the princesses of the royal house, as well as all nobility and higher notables, and, finally, all the officials and the multitude of people ascended and queued there according to their ranks in order to pay the last respects to their beloved and generally venerated king by laying a piece of sandalwood on the funeral pyre. At the corner of the lower square platform four similar smaller baldachins rise up, closed with gold curtains, in which the Buddhist monks say their Pali prayers during the burning of the fire. In the foreground stands a mast at the summit of which there is a gilded swan which has been fixed there as a lamp-bearer. Around the edifice there is a wide corridor, closed on the outside of the building, in which the whole Court as well as the funeral followers attend the celebration. In

the West, East and North large doors have been made, while the middle of the southern side is occupied by the king's parlor from where a hidden corridor leads to the interior of the palace. The South is, as is known, the side of life and of happiness. That all the buildings are covered with gold can also be explained by the fact that such a cremation complex is called Phra Sumeru, the great mountain in the center of the Indo-Siamese world system, also known as Phu Khao Thong, i.e., golden mount.

Plate 76. Cremation celebrations for Prince Uruphong. The funeral procession with the urn. On the wide beautiful main street of the Dusit Park the funeral procession goes from the Dusit Palace to the cremation site. The procession is flanked by two rows of palace servants dressed in white with their characteristic white cloth caps, who are called *phuok thavada* by the people, i.e., troops of angels. Further behind them go in long rows, in red clothes embroidered with gold, the troop of the funeral musicians with ancient hand drums, and, at the utmost right front corner of the photo, the funeral conch blower. In the background can be seen the many ceremonial umbrellas. In the midst of them the supreme patriarch of Siam, Prince Vajirian, is carried on a golden throne. Behind him appears the carriage with the urn. A great funeral cortege closes the procession.

Plate 77. Cremation celebrations for Prince Uruphong. The carriage with the urn. In accordance with the rank of the prince this is noticeably smaller than the royal funeral carriage. Three ship-shaped structures on top of each other can be recognized (see **Plate 78**). Four ceremonial umbrellas each of five stories rise up on the corners. While the long ropes of the great royal funeral carriage were pulled normally by servants, for this funeral horses were harnessed; this goes back to ancient Siamese customs and traditions. On both sides, gold coats of arms hanging from poles are carried, one each, by seven officials who represent the golden flower bushes of the royal funeral procession. The prayer thread, which comes out of the urn, can be especially clearly seen on this photo.

Plate 78. At the cremation ceremony of King Chulalongkorn, March 1911. The funeral procession with the gold urn containing his ashes on the royal funeral carriage. The usual five and seven-layered ceremonial umbrellas are carried in front and behind the funeral carriage. Obviously it has the shape of a ship. In order to honor the king, three such ships, each slightly smaller than the previous, are placed over each other. Above this the tower-shaped superstructure, under which the gold urn stands, rises up. All insignia of the position, which the king wore or carried during his life when he made a public appearance and in festive processions also accompany the body on its way to the funeral pyre. One can see high-ranking palace officials holding the very characteristic royal umbrellas and fans on both sides of the urn and behind it on the carriage.

Plate 79. At the cremation ceremony of King Chulalongkorn, March 1911. Encircling the cremation site with the gold urn with ashes. After the urn with ashes of the king has been placed on the litter, a small procession with the highest-ranking notables walks from the East thrice around the cremation site. In front of the body a son of the king is carried around, sprinkling glutinous rice from a gold bowl. Behind him follows the supreme patriarch on a golden throne. The urn is venerated on the litter itself by two princes in kneeling positions. From the urn with the ashes the wide prayer ribbon run to the praying supreme patriarch supported by dumb-bells,. On both sides of the urn gold flower trees are carried on a long pole which can also be seen on both sides of the carriage in **Plate 78**. While a person must always keep on his right side during the three-fold encircling movement of temples, the *phra chedi*, Buddha images, holy trees and other venerable holy items, here the cremation building is encircled from the left because a right turn means life and a left turn death. The European uniforms of the retinue stand in contradistinction to the ancient Oriental splendor. In the photo the ceremonial umbrella, which for the dead king rises up in nine layers, is clearly recognizable while for living persons it consists of only seven storeys.

Plate 80. At the cremation ceremony of King Chulalongkorn, March 1911. The urn is taken down from the carriage. The funeral procession arrives from the palace before the eastern door of the Phramen building. The whole procession stops there. On the side they have placed a steep sliding device and moved the urn under the baldachin of the carriage onto the side platform. The official of the Ministry of the Royal Household who has been designated for this, in a white funeral dress adorned with gold, kneels in front of the urn and respectfully requests it to come down from the platform to the litter. The urn is accompanied by ceremonial umbrellas. The *mondob* of the carriage, which rises in seven layers, is counted as a ceremonial umbrella. As soon as the urn which contains the royal body has been removed from it, a real ceremonial umbrella, made of white cloth adorned with gold, is erected above the high-rising bronze bar. The higher-ranking officials who are involved with the funeral festivities all wear white costumes and wear white caps adorned with gold thread gathered into upright pointed tips. The richly cut images on the royal funeral carriage, which is entirely covered with gold, can be seen very clearly here.

Plate 81. Cremation festivities for two royal princes. The funeral procession has just completed the three-fold encircling of the cremation building. While one of the urns with ashes still stands at the foot of the eastern ascent, the other has risen up via the sliding device to the upper platform. In kneeling position the palace official, using set words, requests the urn to ascend. The person of the deceased is treated as a live being until the cremation.

Only through turning into ashes does the deceased enter Nirvana, according to Siamese concepts.

Plate 82. A view of the cremation installation from the Phu Kao Thong of the Vat Saket temple. Separated by a street from the temple courtyard, on a great place surrounded by trees, the steep building crowned by a *mondob* rises up. The tower-like roof comprises five stories on top of which there is a row of five oval windows into each direction and then still two roof stories so that the total of stories is seven. As always in things Siamese great emphasis is placed on the right number. The buildings as well as the surrounding halls have an entrance in the middle turned to every side of the compass. The description of Captain Werner is applicable to this edifice (see under Cremation). The cremation shown on **Plate 83** has been photographed here. In the foreground one can see the roofs of the monks' quarters of the Vat Saket temple.

Plate 83. Cremation of a body on the open fire in the cremation grounds of the poor near the Vat Saket temple. The main buildings of the temple are situated on the other side of the street facing a great cremation site in the middle of the city. In the foreground a walled substructure rises up on which the funeral pyres for the cremation of the body are erected in the middle of a large building with a very high roof in the shape of a spire. Big doors open towards all four points of the compass. Even here some expenses are incurred, and the poor, who cannot pay these, may deliver their bodies to the appointed employees against payment for the wood for burning. Coffins with bodies are stored in long buildings that look like warehouses, which stretch out along the back of the cremation grounds, with several raised platforms. Almost continuously the bodies are burned on open fires, even if no relatives are present. During my visit the old white-haired guard told me that he had been burning the dead his whole life, more than 40 years. Dense smoke covered the courtyard whilst the employees adjusted the bodies with a long hook. His vacant look and puckered face framed small half closed eyes very inflamed due to the continual burning.

Formerly the bodies of pious Buddhists, who had made this known before their deaths and who could not afford the wood for burning, were thrown to the vultures and dogs as food while the gnawed bones were burned later. Lunet de la Jonquière writes about this in his book *Le Siam et les Siamois* (pages 21-22): "At the foot of the hill, opposite the entrance, a complex of new edifices for cremations rises up in the old courtyard where the dogs and the vultures were thrown the bodies of those who had brought the gift of their mortal remains in order to earn merit. These customs are at present probably abolished in the name of hygiene but a few years ago I could attend one of these ghastly scenes and even today I cannot get rid of the memory of the sight of the moaning, filthy animals attracted by the stench which ate the human body completely, of the tangle of gray feathers, of the eagerly trembling wings, of the long red necks, naked, lacking in feathers, of the birds flying away with their stretched out heads soiled by dirt from the body, snippets of the flesh of the body in their beaks still."

We have to observe that they have planned the building of modern crematoria recently and that the government has indeed already decided on it. Difficulties are still produced by the fact that after a cremation in a modern crematorium the whole body disintegrates to white powder while the Buddhists place great value on having left some undamaged bone relics, as it was reported the case with the burning of the body of the Lord Buddha. For example the right upper eyetooth or also the front bone are considered to be of special value.

Plate 84. A funeral *phra chedi* in the Vat Bopphit-thimuk temple in Bangkok. Cremation can take place in every temple. The main method of conservation for urns containing ashes is to place them in the base of a *phra chedi*. Thus, near many temples we find entire cemeteries with such funeral monuments. It is astonishing how even not-well-to-do families consecrate such memorial edifices to their relatives, bigger or smaller according to the funds used. Those built in the Vat Bophittihimuk temple are really imposing; the great one in the middle on a round base follows the stricter tradition, while the three others on an angular base with square corners are much more attuned to Siamese taste. To be noticed is the gallery of small columns at the round *phra chedi*, which are built in toto very rarely. The small edifice in the foreground is the tabernacle of a temple border marker.

Plate 85. *Phra chedi* group in the Vat Chetuphon temple, Bangkkok. This temple belongs to the greatest and most splendid of the capital. At the left side of the photo we can see a *phra chedi* group which was erected in memory of the first four kings of the present dynasty. The cremation remains of the kings are not kept here. Formerly, it was the custom to erect monuments in the shape of *phra chedi* for famous kings in Siam; sometimes they also did this in order to preserve the memory of a victory or an important historical event. In the middle of the left group of buildings the great, dark blue memorial to the memory of King Mongkut rises up. The spires of the *phra chedi* have been destroyed long ago. At the right side of the photo one can see the library of the monastery built in splendid mosaic incrustation.

Plate 86. Cremation celebrations for Prince Uruphong. An offering of flowers in the shape of an urn for ashes. The Siamese are masters in the production of beautiful flower compositions which are put together especially of white, very fragrant *mali* blossoms—some kind of jasmine. This urn of ashes only consists of blossoms which are held together partly with wax.

Plate 87-102. Buddhism, to which these plates belong, is treated in a special chapter of the third volume.[14] It is sufficient here to add a few short remarks about the plates.

Plate 87-89. According to the Siamese-Buddhist conception it is very meritorious work to build temples, *phra chedi* or Buddha images. The person who does not have such means available suffices with placing at the foot of a *phra chedi* of a Buddha statue a small model of a *phra chedi* or a votive Buddha image as a holy gift. Also very much in favor are the clay-paste tablets shown in these photos. This custom already existed in the oldest Buddhism of early India and at the excavations in Buddha Gaya many such clay-paste tablets were found. In **Plate 87** they are in the shape of *bai sema* or temple border-markers. On both plates are displayed ten Buddha images, by three in three rows above each other while the tenth thrones in the middle, with to the right and the left each one *phra chedi*. On the plate on the left we have the Buddha posture of the Phra Sadung man, who, by using his hand placed on his knee, calls the Earth as a witness against the devil Mara. On the right side the posture of Phra Samathi, who places both hands in his lap and is immersed in mediation, has been selected.

Plate 88 shows a Buddha supported by *sing* in a *phra prang* edifice seated on a throne. To the right and the left there are young Mokhala and Saribut in meditation posture.

The votive tablet shown in **Plate 89** is burned from white clay. The work is much finer than on the preceding tablet and allows one to conclude it is of a greater age. Again Buddha is shown between his two favorite youngsters. To the right and left of them are lay people who offer lotus flower presents. On the various sections of the gable structure one can see another five small Buddhas.

Plate 90. A column gallery of the main building of the Vat Thephsirin temple, Bangkok. The splendid temple buildings of Siam testify to the religious zeal of the inhabitants. They do not consist of a single building only but of a great number of edifices placed together according to a uniform plan. The most important building, the main temple, is especially to serve the monkshood for holding religious celebrations. The roof with multiple layers, a splendidly decorated gable and snake heads standing up in multiples, rises above a forest of lotus columns in full splendor. The gable triangle is adorned with delightful earthenware mosaic.

Plate 91. The Vat Rajabophit temple, Bangkok. In the middle of the whole temple a *phra chedi* covered with yellow glazed earthenware tiles rises up surrounded by a double circular hall for walking around which opens to the inside and outside through rows of pillars. At the four points of the compass, the walking hall is interrupted by four temple structures. Vat Rajabophit is among the most beautiful temples of recent times.

Plate 92-93. Bell towers. In the monastery complexes the monks are called to the occupations and events of the day by ringing bells. They are woken up for the first religious rites very early, later called for the collection of alms, to take the last meal of the day and then to prayers in the evening cool. Instead of the bell they often use a drum or a trumpet.

Plate 94. Buddhist monks with their pupils and servants. The costumes of monks consist of yellow silk or cotton cloth which are given to them by pious laymen. They wrap the cloth around their bodies in such a way that the right arm and the right shoulder are left uncovered and from the left shoulder a long straight fold is left hanging down.

At the age of 15 to 16 years, after the tonsure ceremony, the Siamese formerly entered the monastery as novices (*nen*) and pupils of the monks, dressed in the same yellow robes. In Siam it is still a general custom for young men at the age of 20 years to enter the monastery in order to learn the basic precepts of the religion. Most of them leave again after a few years in order to marry. Many however also stay in the monastery until their last years. Life in the monastery is counted as a special merit. Monks of the strict rites cannot touch money, therefore they mostly have a servant who carries everything and who manages their money. The servant does not wear monk's cloths but the dress of the common people.

Plate 95. A group of Siamese dressed in white at a memorial service for a deceased at the funeral *phra chedi*. White is the color of mourning. The Buddhist nuns are also dressed in white. At cremation ceremonies all mourning people, who are below the deceased in rank or age, appear in white. For a time after the death such mourning celebrations are held more often, later only at six-month or yearly intervals. On these occasions they stick palms in the ground at the funeral *phra chedi* and bring flowers, incense and candle offerings.

Plate 96. Siamese at the building of a sand *phra chedi* in the courtyard of the Vat Anong temple, Bangkok. During the Song Khran celebration, the birthday of Buddha in the winter solstice [*sic*], it is a general custom in Siam to set up small sand *phra chedi* in temple courtyards. Usually one builds 108 *phra chedi* in order to obtain merit. This number occurs in other ways in Buddhism: on the prayer rosary of the monks one finds 108 beads, a really true Buddha footprint is marked by 108 holy marks. One should also remember that the pious Hindu made 108 small *lingam* at the bank of the Ganges from its mud. In these small *phra chedi* they place coins or other small gifts for the priests. In the spires they stick small flags or lotus flowers. In these festivities in the temple courtyards all ranks of people participate, even the king.

Plate 97-98. Meals for the priests in the Vat That-Upanom temple, Vientiane. During the Totkatin celebration the priests are given offerings and food, not only by the king, but also by the nobles and the people. During such a meal the pious laymen bring the monks a meal in the monastery while otherwise they obtain the necessary food during their morning collection of alms. On this occasion the monks are given the most exquisite and choice food. Among the gifts is usually a new yellow robe.

Also at the Krut Thai or Siamese New Year the monks are receiving meals at their temple and rich gifts. During these celebrations Siamese, Lao, Cambodians, Peguans and Burmese compete to fulfill meritorious woks for the Buddhist religion. Special cakes are baked. These and fruits of all kinds are given to the priests. The temples are open during the celebrations and the people, especially women and children come in their best dress and most expensive jewelry and bring the Buddha image offers of flowers, incense and candles. The prominent families invite the priests into their houses where they recite prayers and chants in singing tones. After the religious exercise the priests are rewarded and offered yellow robes and other necessities of life.

Plate 99. Priests during the dry season walkabout with their resting tents. During the rainy season, since time immemorial, Buddhist monks are prohibited to move around. During this time they stay in their monastery and only leave it for the collection of alms or if they are called upon by pious laymen to pray and preach in their houses. However, during the dry season they walk around in the countryside, from town to town, from monastery to monastery, visiting especially famous temples and *phra chedi* that are worth venerating. Because they are shaved clean they protect themselves from the rays of the sun by a great white umbrella. On it they have also fixed the mosquito net which is folded on the edge of the umbrella while they walk around. If they rest at a temple they stick the umbrella in the ground, let the mosquito-net drop down and fix the umbrella with a rope to protect it from the wind. Thus are made small, circular tents in which the monks can sleep at night without being bitten by insects.

Plate 101. A Buddha statue in the main building of the Vat Bovoranivet temple, Bangkok. This is an old, famous statue from the north of the country, which has been put on display here. The Buddha niche has been closed by a curtain, behind which a second, larger statue has been erected. On both sides stand bronze statues of the two favorite young men in the venerating position. In front of the Buddha image have been displayed flower offerings, incense and candles on altars as well as other gifts, paintings, vases and small Buddha statuettes.

Plate 102. A gilded bronze Buddha statue. It is a peculiarity of Siamese Buddhism to depict the Buddha statue in full royal dress. The jewelry is very rich but is still completely similar to present-day jewelry worn by kings, nobles and princes during festive occasions as can be seen in the next plate.

Plate 103. A Siamese prince made up for the tonsure ceremony. The young prince is sitting on a splendid gold throne completely overloaded with gold jewelry and brilliants. On both sides are placed on small tables the attributes of his power, on the right side a tea set, bottles with holy water and the sword, on the left the betel nut set, the spittoon and the saber. The legs of the table are supported by snakes, similarly, the armrests of the throne chair end in multiple snake heads. The person depicted is a son of King Chulalongkorn and his main queen, thus a so-called "Heavenly Prince."

Plate 106. King Chulalongkorn as a prince. He wears the usual dress of the Siamese, the *pha nung*. His torso is covered with a brocade jacket with a tight pattern; around the waist he has wrapped a waistcloth (*pha rataeo*). He is still before the tonsure ceremony because he wears a garland of flowers around his hair tuft. His ankles are adorned with heavy foot buckles. Next to him on the table stand a teapot and a betel-box.

Plate 112. Edifice for the tonsure ceremony for a royal prince in the courtyard of the city palace, Bangkok. The large, palace-like entirely gilded edifice has been erected for the day of the ceremony only as has the rocky hill on which it stands and after the celebration they will be demolished. The whole edifice is surrounded by seven-layered ceremonial umbrellas.

Plate 113. Arrangements for the festive parade at the tonsure ceremony for two royal princes. In front are displayed the two princes on their throne-like chairs with their accompanying retinue. On the balcony-like jutting structure King Chulalongkorn stands under an umbrella. In the background one can see the door to the interior palace in which the women of the king live. Many of them look out from the windows to take part.

Plate 120. A procession of ships on the water at a Court celebration. On the river a floating, splendid festive palace has been moored to hold the ceremony, surrounded by many seven-layered ceremonial umbrellas. A whole flotilla of long royal barges is displayed in a procession on the river. Many of them have the shapes of dragons, for example the boat displayed in **Plate 117**, ends at the front in a seven-layered snake and dragon-heads. The boatsmen are trained to sink the oars into the water and lift them out in unison. The oars are gilded for many boats and these splendid oars moving in cadence and glittering in the sunlight are a delightful sight. Already centuries ago the boat processions of the kings of Siam were famous. [...]

Plate 121. Provisional palace erected to the memory of the 40th anniversary of the reign of King Chulalongkorn. After the destruction of Ayuthia in 1767 the capital was not rebuild by King Phya Tak. However, after the liberation of the country he went to the ruins of the old capital and slept one night in his tent in the compound of the destroyed palace. King Chulalongkorn had the longest reign among all kings (42 years). Under his predecessors the longest time was 36 years. When he reigned 40 years a great feast was held. For this a provisional palace was built on the foundations of the old palace in Ayuthia in which the king lived only for a few days during the celebration. Then the splendid proud building disappeared from the face of the Earth.

Plate 122. The great earth dragon of the festive parade at the anniversary of King Chualongkorn's reign in 1908. Many ministries as well as the great merchants and the population of Bangkok celebrated this feat by a great festive parade, which went on passing in front of the royal pavilion from 9 a.m. until 6 p.m. with a small noon time break. The Ministry of Agriculture symbolically represented the Earth by a huge, almost 100 meter long snake which consisted solely of small carriages tied together with articulations under the imitation skin and which was pulled from the inside by Chinese coolies. The god of the Earth was riding on the snake.

Plate 123. Festive arch for the festivities at the return of King Chulalongkorn from his European journey in 1907. Each of his ministries had collected money by contributions from its officials in order to built honorary arches under which the king would travel on his return to the city. The War Ministry had built this elephant gate which shows the battle between the king of Siam and the king of Burma for the mastery of Indochina. The elephants, much greater than life-size, are shown very faithful to nature and are noteworthy, as are the displays of weapons on the elephants' howdahs, because they are historic. Besides the two kings one can see the two mahouts, one behind the ears and the other behind the saddle. Also these edifices were built only for a few days use.

Plate 126. A group of Siamese theater players. The staging of the fight of Hanuman with Totsakan, The Siamese professional players, who are shown here, wear foot buckles in addition to their extraordinary rich clothes. The embroidery on the apron of the giant king Totsakan depicts the giant Rahu who swallowed the moon. The pretty moving silhouettes of the battle scenes are derived from paintbrush images as they are commonly used as illustrations for the stage scripts in Siam.

Plate 127. Siamese theater players. Totsakan with his wife Nang Munro. The giant king Totsakan usually has a green body color, however when he feels happy in his palace, he is also depicted with a gold mask. The ten heads of the giant noble are arranged in three layers above each other and in such a way that at the back three more faces are placed. Above this there is another head, which shows four faces; the highest head is a Janus face. While all other faces are demonic with pig teeth, the front one is human on top. The giant king carries as his weapon a bludgeon, which is inset with a mirror glass mosaic.

The female player of the woman's role is made up to have a snow-white face and like most theater players she wears a bundle of artfully tied up flowers on the left side of her face.

Plate 128. Siamese ballet. The scenic background with side-wings and a building are unusual. Half of the twelve players are wearing male costumes with a *pha nung* while the others wear the *pha sin*, a long dress falling down and which is similar to our ladies' underskirts. Here is displayed a long, common, synchronized dance.

Plate 129. A Siamese theater troop with a musical orchestra. The photo does not show scenes but all the members of the troop have gathered to display a picturesque composition. In the foreground one can see on the right side both kettle drums and the gong hanging from a tripod; on the left there is a circular battery of gongs in the middle of which the player is seated, and hand timpani. Under two great banana trees the various theater players are standing and sitting; among them one can recognize Phya Krut with the bird feathers. In front of him is the god Phra In with green facial paint.

Plate 130. A love scene. With inimitable grace these two figures have entwined themselves. Especially beautiful and expressive is the elegant hand language.

Plate 131. The farewell scene from *Inao*. The play *Inao* is the Siamese version of the Dido saga. Shown is the farewell of the hero. The facial expression of the female lead shows her anguish and great bitterness. Noteworthy are especially the long, silver, bent fingernails of the theater player and the strong bending of the left arm of the hero, which strikes us at first as unnatural but among the Siamese this is demanded from theater players. They call such a body posture *on*, i.e., supple, and our European postures hard. Both theater players have their faces made up brightly.

Plate 132. A prominent Siamese woman in a theater costume. The theater player depicts a male role. Her costume has been overloaded with precious stones and brilliants. Especially characteristic is the play of the finger. In Siamese theater there is a fixed language of movements and finger expressions. Noteworthy is once more the flower bouquet which, according to a Siamese superstition, brings the theater player success and hangs down from the crown on the right side.

Plate 133. Professional theater players. All three players are made up heavily so that the eyebrows and eyelashes are partly covered with white powder.

Plate 134-135. Prominent Siamese women in theater costumes. The players are overly decorated with gold necklaces, flower compositions, real stones and real gold specks.

Plates 136-139 shows groups of two each prominent Siamese women who perform in house-theaters. In love scenes it is to be expected that the Siamese do not kiss but bring their faces and breath together and thus they take in the smell of the other person.

Plate 140. Shadow-play figures cut from leather: Phra Ram. Museum für Völkerkunde in München, Döhring Collection.

The main hero of the great epic of Ramakien appears here riding on a snake with the royal coat of arms, bow and arrow. The head is framed by an aureole. A rich ornamentation gives the whole figure a uniform calm.

Plate 141. Shadow-play figures cut from leather: Pipek. Museum für Völkerkunde in München, Döhring Collection. From the same series of shadow-play figures as the previous plate. The giant Pipek is plump and clumsy in contrast to the slender King Phra Ram. He is carrying the giant's usual weapon, the bludgeon. His skin is covered by small pumpkin crowns. He too, like many figures in shadow-plays, goes around riding on a snake. Characteristic for the giant is the fat tuberous nose, the wide mouth and the upper teeth. He is a brother of the giant king Totsakan. Because he can see into the future, being an astrologer, he warns his brother of a war with Phra Ram. The latter however in his blindness rejects him. As a vagrant he joins the army of King Phra Ram to whom he offered important services as an astrologer, in many dangers. As a reward for these he becomes king of Langka after the death of Totsakan.

Plate 142. Shadow-play figures: Hanuman and Banjakai. Hanuman, the general of the monkey troops, is not only a great, victorious hero, rich in tricks, but also the hero of a lot of romantic adventures. Benjakai is the daughter of the giant king Totsakan. She is sent out by her father in order to scare away Phra Ram and his army from a war against Langka by a trick. The deceit goes wrong and she is captured. Hanuman is given the order to punish her. When she has sat out the punishment, he leads her back and falls in love with her. She too offers her love to him. But duty calls Hanuman to the battle and he promises her, like so many others, that when the war is over he will come back and bring her to his home.

Notes

[1] With a new king the national coat of arms also changes in Siam.

[2] Bangkok has had water piping and sewerage drains for about ten years.

[3] The wood of *Caesalpina sappan*, also called Brazil wood, but really assumed to be originally from Siam and Champa and exported to Europe since the Middle Ages. (Tran. note)

[4] A tower-like edifice with a strongly elongated spire (see below). (Tran. note)

[5] This title is not conferred generally anymore, only in the Ministry of the Royal Household.

[6] Presently, there is indeed also a *Mom Luang* rank between *Mom Rajawong* and *Nai*. (Tran. note)

[7] That serfdom—although it was certainly not European-style plantation slavery—had negative consequences and was not free from occasional abuse is illustrated in the review of law cases contained in *Crime and Punishment in King Chulalongkorn's Kingdom. The Special Commission for the Reorganisation of the Provincial Courts in Ayuthia (1896-1897)*, White Lotus, 1998. (Tran. note)

[8] This is done to avoid that the dead returns and haunts and harms the inhabitants of the house. However, the remembrance of the original purpose has mostly disappeared.

[9] White and black are mourning colors in Siam but white mostly as a color of the West.

[10] The above description is only one among many since funerals varied greatly. Other authors have given further details and explanations of some of the symbolic acts in funerals, see e.g. in Charles Buls, *Siamese Sketches*, White Lotus, 1994, and, especially, Mr. & Mrs. E. Jottrand's *In Siam. The Diary of a Legal Adviser of King Chulalongkorn's Government*, White Lotus, 1996. (Tran. note)

[11] The Chakkri dynasty presently reigning has a throwing quoit and a trident in their coat of arms.

[12] Additional details on many of the following descriptions as well as some corrections and other interpretations are given in Lucien Fournereau's interesting description, *Bangkok in 1892*, White Lotus, 1999. (Tran. note)

[13] Charles Buls and Mr. and Mrs. E. Jottrand, *op. cit.*, present descriptions and photos of some of the more common expressions of this art. (Tran. note)

[14] The author refers to his seminal three-volume work, *Buddhistische Tempelanlagen in Siam*. Berlin 1920. (Tran. note)

1. A canal scene in the vicinity of Bangkok
Kanalszene in der Nähe von Bangkok

2. Canal in the Menam Plain
Kanal in der Menam-Ebene

3. A canal near Bangkok with a temple entrance
Kanal bei Bangkok mit Eingang zu einem Tempel

4. A view of Bangkok
Blick auf Bangkok

5. A canal near Wat Rajabophit, Bangkok, with a view of the royal cemetery
Kanal beim Tempel Vat Rajabphit (Blick auf den Prinzenfriedhof). Bangkok

6. A Siamese in one of the customary small rowing-boats
Siamese in einem der gebräuchlichen kleinen Ruderboote

7. Siamese disembarking at a temple in the vicinity of Bangkok
Siamesen, bei einem Tempel in der Nähe von Bangkok landend

69

8. A canal scene in Bangkok during low tide
Kanalszene in Bangkok zur Zeit der Ebbe

70

9. A canal scene in Bangkok Noi at market time
Kanaszene in Bangkok Noi zur Marktzeit

10. Traffic on a canal in Bangkok Noi
Verkehr auf einem Kanal in Bangkok Noi

11. Pilgrims in boats at the Phra Chedi Klang Nam
Pilger in Booten bei dem Phrachedi Klang Nam

12. A settlement of Siamese on a canal in the Menam Plain
Siamesen-Niederlassung an einem Kanal in the Menam-Ebene

13. A Siamese house on stilts on a canal in Bangkok Noi
Siamesisches Pfahlhaus an einem Kanal in Bangkok Noi

14. Siamese house on stilts in the countryside near Bangkok
Siamesisches Pfahlhaus auf dem Lande bei Bangkok

15. A floating house on the Menam near Bangkok
Schwimmendes Haus auf dem Menam bei Bangkok

16. Houseboats and floating houses near Tha Sa
Wohnboote und schwimmende Häuser bei Tha Sa

17. A Canal in Ayuthia with floating houses on bamboo rafts and houseboats
Kanal in Ayuthia mit schwimmenden Häusern auf Bambusflößen und Hausbooten

18a. A floating market on the river near Bangkok
Bootmarkt auf dem Strom bei Bangkok

18b. Large houseboats on the Menam in Upper Siam
Große Hausboote auf dem Menam in Obersiam

19. A houseboat on the Menam River in Upper Siam
Hausboot auf dem Menamstrom in Obersiam

20. Canal scenery with a sailing rice boat near the village of Klong Rangsit
Kanallandschaft mit segelndem Reisboot bei dem Dorf Khlong Rangsit

21. A houseboat on a canal in the Menam Plain
Hausboot auf Kanal in der Menam-Ebene

22. Mountain scenery in the vicinity of Khao Phyng
Gebirgslandschaft in der Nähe des Khao Phyng

23. A view of the mountain temple in the vicinity of the old fortifications in Petchaburi
Blick auf den Bergtempel in der Nähe des alten Schlosses in Petchaburi

24. Siamese performing a dance play. On the left women, on the right men
Siamesen bei einem Tanzspiel. Links Frauen, rechts Männer

25. Felons cast in chains
Schwerverbrecher, in Eisen geschlossen

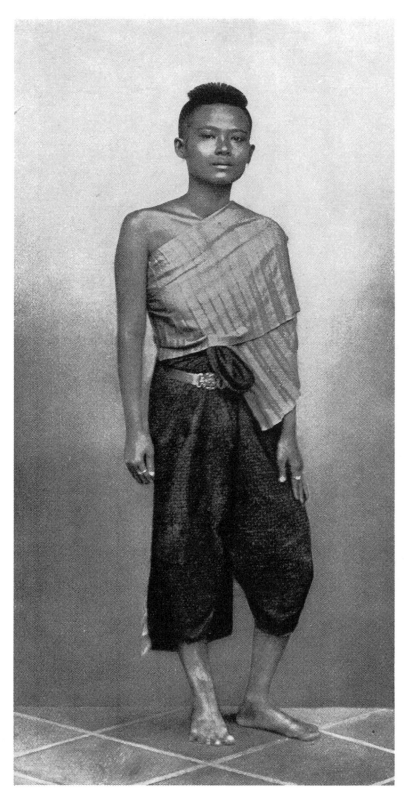

26. A Siamese woman from King Mongkut's time (1851-1868)
Siamesin aus der Zeit des Königs Mongkut (1851-1868)

27. An oarsman from King Mongkut's time
Ruderer aus der Zeit des Königs Mongkut

28. A high-ranking Siamese from King Mongkut's time
Vornehme Siamesin aus der Zeit des Königs Mongkut

29. Two Siamese from King Chulalongkorn's time (1868-1910)
Zwei Siamesinnen aus der Zeit des Königs Chulalongkorn (1868-1910)

30. A Siamese, Bangkok
Siamesin, Bangkok

31. A bathing Siamese
Badende Siamesin

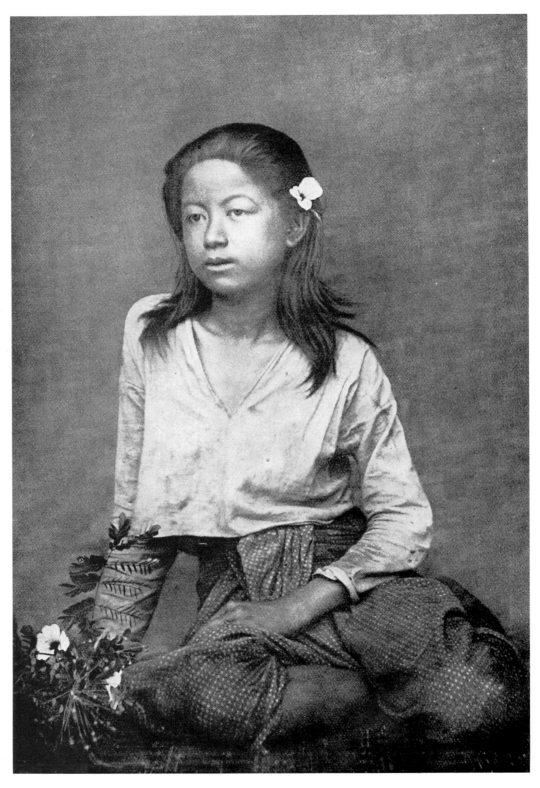

32. A Mon girl from the vicinity of Bangkok
Monmädchen aus der Nähe von Bangkok

33. An old Laotian with her grandchild
Alte Laotin mit Enkelkind

34. Laotian women resting near Utaradit
Laotinnen auf der Rast bei Utaradit

35. Laotian women from Muang Payap
Laotinnen aus Myang Payap

36. A Laotian woman on the weaving loom, Phitsanulok Province
Laotin am Webestuhl, Provinz Pitsanulok

37. Laotian women husking rice, Pitsanulok Province
Laotinnen beim Reisenthülsen. Provinz Pitsamulok

38. Laotian women from Muang Payap
Laotinnen aus Myang Payap

39. A fishing Laotian
Laote beim Fischen

40. Laotian woman
Laotin

41. Laotian woman
Laotin

42. A Laotian house, with an oxen carriage in front
Laotenhaus, davor Ochsengefährt. Petchaburi

43. An oxen carriage, North Siam
Ochsenwagen, Nordsiam

44. Kha people, hill tribes from North Siam, armed with crossbows
Mit Armbrüsten bewaffnete Kha-Leute, Bergbewohner Nordsiams

45. Karen people from the mountains of the Lao countries
Karen-Leute aus den Bergen der Laos-Staaten

46. Women of a Kha tribe from Muang Payap
Frauen eines Kha-Stammes aus Myang Payap

47. Karen women from the mountains of the Lao countries
Karen-Frauen aus den Bergen des Laos-Staaten

48. A woman from Muang Payap
Frau aus Myang Payap

49. A woman from Muang Payap
Frau aus Myang Payap

50. A Karen woman
Karen-Frau

51. A Karen woman
Karen-Frau

52. Karen people from the mountains of the Lao countries, North Siam
Karen-Leute aus den Bergen der Laos-Staaten, Nordsiam

53. Karen from Northwest Siam
Karen aus dem Nordwesten Siams

54. A Karen playing the Lao flute
Karen, die Laosflöte spielend

55. A girl from a Kha tribe of North Siam
Mädchen eines Kha-Stammes aus Nordsiam

56. A ox caravan of the Shan climbs over the Khao Phyng pass
Eine Ochsenkarawane der Shan ünberklettert den Paß des Khao Phyng

57. A Siamese farmstead of North Siam (Pitsanulok Province)
Siamesen-Gehöft aus Nordsiam (Provinz Pitsanulok)

119

58. Ploughing of the rice fields with water buffaloes
Das Pflügen der Reisfelder mit Wasserbüffeln

59. Siamese planting rice
Siamesen beim Reis-Pflanzen

60. Market boats with corn cobs
Marktboote mit Maiskolben

122

61. Siamese women sell bananas, coconuts and areca nuts in the market, Phrapathom

Siamesinnen verkaufen auf dem markt Bananen, Kokos- und Areka-Nüsse. Phrapathom

62a. A festive parade of the Laotians, Petchaburi
Festzug des Laoten. Petchaburi

62b. A resting elephant with its mahout
Ruhender Elefant mit Kornak

63. An elephant caravan in the jungle
Elefantenkarawane im Dschungel

64. Departing elephants
Elephanten beim Abmarsch

65. Caparisoned elephants with princes in the courtyard of the Royal Palace in Bangkok
Aufgezäumte Elefanten mit Prinzen auf dem Hof des kgl. Palastes zu Bangkok

66. A Royal Elephant in the Saranrom Garden
Kgl. Elefant im Saranrom-garten

67. A work elephant transporting teak logs
Arbeitselefant, Teakholzbalken transportierend

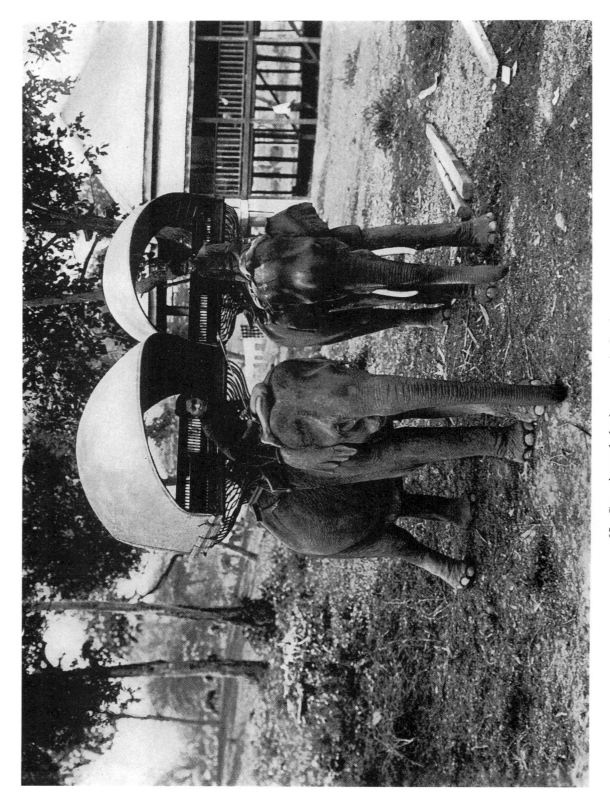

68. Caparisoned elephants, ready for departure
Aufgezäumte Elefanten, fertig zum Aufbruch

69. An elephant caravan crossing a watercourse
Elefantenkarawane, einen Wasserlauf überschreitend

70. War elephants of King Chulalongkorn's Reign
Kriegselefanten unter der Regierung des Königs Chulalongkorn

71. War elephants of King Mongkut's Reign
Kriegselefanten unter der Regierung des Königs Mongkut

72. Edifices for the cremation ceremonies of King Mongkut (deceased 1868)
Aufbau für die Verbrennungsfeierlichkeiten des Königs Mongkut (gest. 1868)

73. View of the edifices for the cremation of royal bodies
Blick auf die Gebäude zur Verbrennung kgl. Leichen

74. Edifices for the cremation of a prince's body in the reign of King Chulalongkorn
Bauten für die Verbrennung der Leiche eines Prinzen unter der Regierung des Königs Chulalongkorn

75. Middle part of the edifices for the cremation ceremonies
of King Chulalongkorn's body, March 1911
*Mittelteil des Baues für die Verbrennungsfeierlichkeiten der Leiche
des Königs Chulalongkorn, März 1911*

76. Funeral procession with the urn of Prinz Urupong
Trauerzug mit der Urne des Prinzen Urupong

77. A gilded carriage with the urn of Prinz Urupong
Vergoldeter Wagen mit der Urne des Prinzen Urupong

78. The carriage with the urn in the cremation ceremonies for King Chulalongkorn's corpse

Von den Verbrennungsfeierlichkeiten für die Leiche des Königs Chulalongkorn. Wagen mit der Urne

79. The thrice repeated procession with the urn of King Chulalongkorn around the cremation site
Dreimaliger Umzug mit der Urne des Königs Chulalongkorn um die Verbrennungsstätte

141

80. Transport of the urn from the carriage to the litter in the cremation ceremonies
for King Chulalongkorn's corpse
Von den Verbrennungsfeierlichkeiten für die Leiche des Königs Chulalongkorn.
Transport der Urne vom Wagen zur Tragbahre

81. Transport of an Urn to the funeral pyre in the cremation ceremonies for two princes
Verbrennungsfeierlichkeiten für zwei Prinzen. Transport einer Urne auf den Scheiterhaufen

82. The cremation installation in the Wat Saket temple, Bangkok
Die Verbrennungsanlage im Tempel Vat Saket, Bangkok

83. Cremation of a corpse on an open fire in the courtyard of the Wat Saket temple, Bangkok
Verbrennung einer Leiche in offenen Feuer im Hof des Tempels Vat Saket, Bangkok

84. A funeral phra chedi in the Wat Bophitthimuk temple, Bangkok
Grabphrachedi im Tempel Vat Bophitthimuk, Bangkok

85. A phra chedi group in the Wat Chetuphin temple, Bangkok
Phrachedigruppe im Tempel Vat Chetuphon, Bangkok

86. A funeral urn decorated with flowers
Aschenurne aus Blumen

87. Fired votive tablets with portrayals of Buddha images
Gebrannte Votivtafeln mit darstellungen von Buddhabildern

88. Gilded fired votive tablets with a Buddha image
Vergoldete, gebrannte Votivtafeln mit Buddhadarstellung

89. Fired votive tablets with a Buddha image
Gebrannte Votivtafeln mit Buddhadarstellung

90. The columned hall of the main building in the Wat Thephsirin temple
Säulenhalle des Hauptgebädes im Tempel Vat Thephsirin

91. The Wat Rajabophit temple, Bangkok
Tempel Vat Rajabophit, Bangkok

92. Bell tower
Glockenturm

93. Bell tower in the Wat Phra Këo temple, Bangkok
Glockenturm im Tempel Vat Phra Këo, Bangkok

94. Two Buddhist monks with a pupil and servants
Zwei buddhistische Mönche mit Schüler und Dienern

95. A group of Siamese dressed in white at the funeral phra chedi for the commemorative devotional of a deceased
Gruppe von weißgekleideten Siamesen bei einer Erinnerungsandacht für einen Verstorbenen am Grabphrachedi

96. Siamese at the casting of sand phra chedi in the courtyard of the Wat Anong Temple, Bangkok
Siamesen beim Bau kleiner Sandphrachedi im Hofe des Tempels Vat Anong, Bangkok

97. Feeding of the priests in the Wat That Upanom temple, Vientiane
Die Speisung von Priestern im Tempel Vat That Upanom, Viengchan

98. Feeding the priests in the Wat That Upanom temple, Vientiane
Die Speisung von Priestern im Tempel Vat That Upanom, Viengchan

160

99. Priests during the dry season with their tent, resting during their wanderings
Priester, während der trockenen Jahreszeit mit ihren Zelten auf der Wanderschaft rastend

100. Several Buddha statues in the Wang Na royal museum, Bangkok
Verschiedene Buddhastatuen in kgl. Museum Vang Na, Bangkok

101. Buddha statue in the main building of the Wat Bovoranivet temple, Bangkok
Buddhastatue im Hauptgebäude des Tempels Vat Bovoranivet, Bangkok

102. Gilded bronze Buddha statue
Vergoldete Buddhastatue aus Bronze

103. A royal prince adorned for the tonsure ceremony
Königlicher Prinz, für die Haarschneidezeremonie geschmückt

104. A royal prince adorned for the tonsure ceremony
Königlicher Prinz, für die Haarschneidezeremonie geschmückt

105. A child of a high-ranking Siamese family adorned for the tonsure feast
Kind aus vornehmer Siamesenfamilie, für die Haarschneidefest geschmückt

106. King Chulalongkorn as prince
König Chulalongkorn als Prinz

107. King Chulalongkorn on the throne in Siamese coronation robes
König Chulalongkorn im siamesischen Krönungsornat auf dem Thron

108. A young prince in King Mongkut's reign
Junger Prinz unter der Regierung des Königs Mongkut

109. A prince dressed in a white, gold embroidered ceremonial robe
Prinz, in einen weißen, goldgestickten Zeremonienmantel gekleidet

110. A Siamese noble man dressed for the Ceremony of the Water of Allegiance
Siamesischer Adliger, für das Fest des Wassers der Treue gekleidet

111. One of the four main wives of King Chulalongkorn
Eine der vier Hauptfrauen des Königs Chulalongkorn

112. Edifice for the celebration of the tonsure ceremony for royal princes in the courtyard
of the city palace of Bangkok
*Aufbau zur Abhaltung der Haarschneidezeremonie für königliche Prinzen im Hofe
des Stadtpalastes zu Bangkok*

113. Arrangement for the procession for the tonsure ceremony of two royal princes
Aufstellung des Festzuges für die Haarschneidezeremonie zweier königlicher Prinzen

114. King Mongkut visits the Wat Chetuphon temple during the Totkatin Celebration
König Mongkut besucht während des Totkatin-Festes den Tempel Vat Chetuphon

115. From a Totkatin procession in the reign of the present King Rama VI
Aus einem Totkatin-Festzug unter der Regierung des jetzigen Königs Rama VI

116. King Chulalongkorn in the Totkatin procession in the neighborhood of Wat Bovoranivet
König Chulalongkorn im Totkatin-Festzug in der Nähe des Tempels Vat Bovoranivet

117. King Chulalongkorn in his parade boat during a Totkatin procession on the water
König Chulalongkorn in seinen Prunkboot während einer Totkatin-Prozession zu Wasser

118. Royal boats in front of the Wat Chetuphon temple during the Totkatin festivities
Kgl. Boote vor dem tempel Vat Chetuphon während der Totkatin-Feierlichkeiten

119. Royal rowing boats during a Totkatin procession
Kgl. Ruderboote während einer Totkatin-Prozession

120. Royal boat parade on the water during a court celebration
Kgl. Schiffsprozession auf dem Wasser bei einer Hoffeier

121. Provisional palace, erected in commemoration of King Chulalongkorn's fortieth government jubilee
Provisorischer Palast, errichtet zur Erinnerung an das 40jährige Regierungsjubiläum des Königs Chulalongkorn

122. The great dragon from the parade for King Chulalongkorn's government jubilee, 1908
Die große Erdschlange aus dem Festzuge zum Regierungsjubiläum des Königs Chulalongkorn, 1908

123. An honorary arch erected for the festivities of King Chulalongkorn's return from his European journey, 1907
Ehrentor, errichtet für die Festlichkeiten bei der Rückkehr des Königs Chulalongkorn von seiner Europareise, 1907

124. A group from a parade
Gruppe aus einem Festzug

125. Dancing in the courtyard of the royal palace during a tonsure ceremony for a royal prince
Tanz im Hofe des kgl. Palastes bei einer Haarschneidezeremonie königlicher Prinzen

126. A troop of Siamese theater actors. The portrayal of a fight between Hanuman and Totsakan
Gruppe siamesischer Schauspieler. Darstellung eines Kampfes Hanumans mit Totsakan

127. Siamese theater actors. Totsakan with Nang Munto, his wife
Siamesische Schauspieler. Totsakan mit seiner Gemahlin Nang Munto

128. Siamese ballet
Siamesisches Ballett

129. A Siamese theater troop with a band
Siamesische Theatertruppe mit Musikkapelle

191

130. Love scene
Liebesszene

131. Farewell scene of "I nao"
Abschiedszene aus "I nao"

132. High-ranking Siamse in a theater dress. Male role
Vornehme Siamesin im Theaterkostüm. Männliche Rolle

133. Professional theater actors
Berufsschauspieler

134. High-ranking Siamese in theater dress. Male role
Vornehme Siamesin im Theaterkostüm. Männliche Rolle

135. High-ranking Siamese in theater dress. Leading role
Vornehme Siamesin im Theaterkostüm. Hauptdarstellerin

136. Love scene
Liebesszene

137. Love scene
Liebesszene

138. Theater scene
Theaterszene

139. A dance in a theater scene
Tanz bei einer Theaterszene

140. Shadowplay figure. King Rama
Schattenspielfigur. König Rama
(Museum für Völkerkunde München, Sammlung Döhring)

141. Shadowplay figure. Phipek
Schattenspielfigur. Phipek
(Museum für Völkerkunde München, Sammlung Döhring)

142. Shadowplay figure. Hanuman and Benjakai
Schattenspielfigur. Hanuman und Benjakai
(Museum für Völkerkunde München, Sammlung Döhring)

Bibliography

ANTONIO, J. Guide-Book of Bangkok and Siam. Bangkok 1904.

BASTIAN, A. Die Völker des östlichen Asien. Band III: Reisen in Siam. Jena 1867.

BOWRING, J. The Kingdom and People of Siam. London 1857.

CRAWFURD, J. Journal of an Embassy from the Governor General of India to the Courts of Siam and Cochin-China. London 1828.

DE CHAUMONT. Relation de l'Ambassade de Mr. le Chevalier de Ch. à la Cour du Roy de Siam. Paris 1686.

DE CHOISY Journal de Voyage de Siam fait en 1685-1686, par Monsieur l'Abbé de Ch. Paris 1687.

DE LA LOUBÈRE Du Royaume de Siam par Monsieur de la Loubère, Envoyé extraordinaire du Roy auprès du Roy de Siam en 1687-1686. Paris 1691.

DILOCK, PRINZ VON SIAM. Die Landwirtschaft in Siam. Leipzig 1908.

DÖHRING, K. Buddhistische Tempelanlagen in Siam. Berlin 1920.

FINLAYSON, G. The Mission to Siam and Hué, the Capital of Cochin China in the Years 1821-22. London 1827.

FOURNEREAU, L. Le Siam ancien I, II. Annales du Musée Guimet. Paris 1895, 1908.

GERVAISE, NICOLAS Histoire naturelle et politique du Royaume de Siam. Paris 1688.

GRÜNWEDEL, A. Buddhistische Kunst in Indien. 2. Auflage. Berlin 1900.

HESSE-WARTEGG, E. VON Siam, das Land des Weißen Elefanten. Leipzig 1899.

LEONOWENS, ANNA HARRIETTE The English Governess at the Siamese Court. Boston 1873.

LUNET DE LAJONQUIÈRE, CT. E. Le Siam et les Siamois. Paris 1906.

PALLEGOIX, J. B. Description du royaume Thai ou Siam. Paris 1854.

PINTO, F. M. Fernand Pinto's abenteuerliche Reise durch China, die Tartarei, Siam, Pegu und andere Länder des östlichen Asiens. Neu bearbeitet von Ph. H. Külb. Jena 1868.

SCHOUTEN, DESCRIPTIO REGNI SIAM Per Iodocum Schoutenium qui anno 1636 haec scripsit Belgico sermone. Translata in Latinum per Bernhardum Varenium. Constitutes part of the Collective work: Descriptio regni Japoniae cum quibusdam affinis materiae ex variis auctoribus collectae et ordinem redacta per Bernhardum Varenium. Med. D. Amstelodami, Apud Ludovicum Elzevirium. Anno 1649.

Smyth, H. Warington Five Years in Siam, from 1891 to 1896. 2 Vols. London 1898.

Reinhold, Werner Die Expeditionen nach China, Japan und Siam in 1860, 61, 63. Leipzig 1863.

Spiess, Gustav. Die Preußische Expedition nach Ostasien während der Jahre 1860-62. Berlin-Leipzig, 1864.

Stumpf, Carl Tonsystem und Musik der Siamesen. Beiträge zur Akustik und Musikwissenschaft, Heft III. Leipzig 1906.

Tachard, Guy Voyage de Siam de P.P. Jesuites envoyés par le Roi. Paris 1686.

Thomson, P. A. Lotus Land Being an Account of the Country and the People of the Southern Siam. London 1906

Van Ravenswaay, L. F. Jeremias van Vliet's Description of the Kingdom of Siam. Journal of the Siam Society, Volume VII, Part I. Bangkok 1910.